How to Jump Without a Parachute

A journey to lead with purpose in work and life

Henry Smith

© 2023, Henry Smith

All rights reserved. No part of this book may be reproduced in any form or by any means, electronic or mechanical, including photocopying, recording or by any information or retrieval, without prior permission in writing from the publisher. Under the Australian Copyright Act 1968 (the Act), a maximum of one chapter or 10 per cent of the book, whichever is the greater, may be photocopied by any educational institution for its educational purposes provided that the education institution (or the body that administers it) has given a remuneration notice to Copyright Agency Limited (CAL) under the Act.

From *Bossypants* by Tina Fey, copyright © 2011. Reprinted by permission of Reagan Arthur Books, an imprint of Hachette Book Group, Inc.

A CIP catalogue of this book is available from the National Library of Australia.

Smith, Henry
How to Jump Without a Parachute

ISBN 978-0-646-87600-9

Published by Taste Creative Pty Ltd
Suite 1, Level 10, 76 Berry Street, North Sydney, NSW, 2060

Editing by Jessica Stewart
Proofreading by Angela Damis
Illustrations by Henry Smith

For enquiries, contact hello@tastecreative.com
www.tastecreative.com

Upon the theatrical release of *The Fabelmans*, Steven Spielberg said that if he only had the chance to make just one more movie, *The Fabelmans* would be it. The story of his start.

If I could share just one story with my young self, this book would be it. The story I wish I had at the start.

With grateful thanks to my three ladies
Genevieve, Monet and Everest

You are my reason to lead with authenticity

Contents

An Introductory Note   01
No advice, sorry   03

PART ONE
Purpose

01 ORIGINS OF PURPOSE
The Entire Course of My Life Changed When I Was
Fifteen Years Old   13

02 PERSONAL PURPOSE
Your Purpose Is Bigger Than You   25

03 PURPOSE VS PROFIT
Purpose Isn't a Slap of Paint on the Outside   35

PART TWO
Purposeful Life

04 COURAGE
My Best Friend Gave Me the Greatest Gift of All   51

05 A START
Create a Space Just Your Size   61

06 STARTUP
How to Jump Without a Parachute   83

07 BENEFITING OTHERS
The Earth Didn't Tremble But the World Changed   109

PART THREE
Leading with Purpose

08 LEADING
Leadership Came Naturally, But to Do It
Well Was Another Thing Altogether   125

09 CULTURE
I Once Met Bad Culture; She's a Middle-Aged Film
Producer Driving a Porsche Convertible, and She
Doesn't Give Two Rats About You   139

10 PEOPLE
Art Is a Team Sport   151

11 VALUES
I Knew We Were Doing Something
Right When a Colleague Called Me Out   167

12 SUPPORTING THE TEAM
Learning How to Get The Eggs   177

13 BALANCE
A Jar of Rocks Changed My Life   189

PART FOUR
Purpose at Work

14 MOUNTAINS AND VALLEYS
This Was the Hardest Decision
I Ever Had to Make   205

15 HONOURING FAILURE
Everyone Deserves the Right to Fail   217

16 MANIPULATION VS MOTIVATION
How We Increased Viewership by 14,000%   231

17 STORYTELLING
Great Leaders Are Storytellers   241

18 CHARTING A COURSE
Without a Destination, I Nearly Ran Aground   249

19 MISSION DRIFT
The Man Who Chases Two Rabbits,
Catches Neither   257

20 CREATIVE SURVIVAL
Learning How to Live. Really Live.   265

Acknowledgments   273
About the Author   277

An Introductory Note

The journey, the insights and the lessons shared in this book are experienced regularly, but not often discussed—so everyone repeats and learns the hard way.

Most readers will still do some of that, but let these learnings help with the signs and the traps.

The core of this story is the leadership journey. None of us come fully formed as leaders. Some of us have key attributes and ingredients ... Henry is one of those people. His energy balances his humility, his ambition balances his empathy, his purpose drives him to be his best and his partnership with Gen balances his world.

This book is a great insight into Henry's very human journey—so far!

Ann Sherry AO
Chairman UNICEF Australia
Chancellor Queensland University of Technology
Director National Australia Bank

No advice, sorry

Like so many people around the world, in 2020 I was forced to stop and rethink everything that I knew.

In a year that will be remembered in history, Covid-19 sunk its claws into society and dramatically altered our way of living. British journalist Oliver Burkeman called the pandemic's impact on society at large 'The Great Pause'. It was a forced change of pace for our busy lives—we went from having control over so much within our schedules, to having to change and adapt, often against our will.

Nearly everyone I spoke to shared a guilty delight that, in amongst a lot of difficulty and pain, they were really enjoying the enforced pause to slow down, reassess their priorities, spend more time with their family and even find the space to learn new skills; learning how to bake bread was hot favourite amongst friends. Mine was to master the art of a good coffee pour*.

---

* I still haven't managed to master it yet, thanks for asking.

Having the time and headspace to slow down and begin writing this book was an absolute joy. These were insights and stories that I always wanted to share, but never thought I would have the gift of 'The Great Pause' that Covid presented.

At the time that Covid hit our Australian shores in early 2020, I was leading a team of talented permanent and freelance creatives at a film production company I had started with my wife. As the CEO, I was doing my best to steer our company through the challenges of the pandemic. Like countless other businesses, we were hit very hard and gathering our team to share crucial updates became an all-too-frequent occurrence—projects that clients had to delay indefinitely or cancel altogether, our employees job security, changing protocols on our film sets, the health and safety of the team, and the individual impact the pandemic was having on each of them and their families.

After fifteen months of global disruption and uncertainty, all of our projects had stopped indefinitely and we were not sure how we would be able to pay the salaries of our staff (more on that later). We lost all control of our normality at work and had to learn very quickly how to let go. Towards the end of the pandemic my world flipped upside down again as we welcomed the long-awaited arrival of our twin girls, Monet and Everest. As new parents, and with twins no less, we immediately lost all control of our normality at home.

Up to this point, leadership had looked a certain way to me. But it was about to be fundamentally challenged. A level of control had been synonymous with what leading had meant to me, but here we were entering an era where control was not something that we had at our fingertips. But as I began to find my footing, a new dimension of what leadership needed to be started to emerge.

In an interview with *Atomic Habits* author James Clear, he casually shared that, 'We write the books we need.' This is definitely the book I needed at the start of my career. Starting a production company at the tender age of twenty, I always felt I didn't know enough, like I wasn't as good as the others. A classic case of inposter syndrome at its finest. As a teenager, I had dropped out of university halfway through my course (more on that later too) so I always had that niggle in the back of my mind that I didn't know as much as I needed to. So I read and listened a lot. I devoured a copious number of books and podcasts on business, leadership and management, behavioural motivation, time productivity and a never-ending pile of inspirational biographies of great leaders from around the world. And I loved it. I felt motivated, challenged and excited. My poor staff, however, would often be the guinea pigs to test out the new business techniques or time management hacks I was learning that week, until I would read another book and get excited about implementing the next thing.

After many years of this incessant need to learn and self-develop, I got to a point when I had to stop bingeing all of this content. The principles, techniques, strategies and motivators were starting to blur together and lose clarity. I became overwhelmed by all of the things I felt I should be doing, and this just added to the enormous amount of pressure I was already putting on myself to succeed.

This book is the book that I needed back then.

When I was a kid, my dad had a great mate that he would catch up with often. He was a church minister who sang and played guitar in a band that did great Paul Kelly covers and he knew how to tell great stories. He and Dad would go camping together and sit up late reading poetry to each other and laughing at stories. He was a wise man and I liked to talk to him. It almost became a joke, but every time I would see him, we would sit down and I would ask him, you know, man to man, 'What is the meaning of life?' Year after year, I never got a conclusive answer to this question, but he did share his experiences and stories. As a kid, this was terribly frustrating; I wanted a straight answer. But now, as an adult, I am grateful he didn't talk to me like a child back then. He encouraged me to think for myself.

In this book you won't find sure-fire answers that you can go away to implement and it will immediately improve your life. In fact, I intentionally avoid giving advice like this. This mantra is shared in a group called the Entrepreneurs' Organization (EO). Revolving around the sharing of personal and career experiences, EO is for entrepreneurs to self-develop, grow and support each other. And a foundational rule is that members are not allowed to give advice to each other. To the degree that if you do give direct advice to another member in a forum setting, you get one warning before facing the very real probability of being asked to leave. They're serious, and for good reason.

This is because when we give direct advice to each other, it doesn't allow the recipient to discover the best answer for themselves. Solutions aren't always simple and, most often, advice is brittle. An answer that someone else has discovered, no matter how wildly successful they may be, may not always be the right fit for you. Instead, members of EO work with a powerful principle called Gestalt, or Forum Mindset. Simply put, Gestalt means no judgement and no advice, just shared experiences. Shared experiences encourage us to find our own answers, and take ownership of the outcome.

So you won't find advice in this book. But I will share a number of interesting experiences and my hope is that you will find encouragement and inspiration for your own self discovery.

PART ONE

Purpose

CHAPTER ONE | ORIGINS OF PURPOSE

The Entire Course of My Life Changed When I Was Fifteen Years Old

I had a pretty fortunate childhood. Being raised in the Adelaide Hills of South Australia, I grew up in a very beautiful part of the world. We had most of our extended family living within a fifteen-minute drive and my sister and I were brought up in a very supportive household. We were taught the importance of table manners, respect for all people, the value of education and working hard to earn a living. Mum and Dad were both high school teachers, Mum in art and Dad teaching at an agriculture school, so we were lucky to have a pretty cultured upbringing.

As a kid I didn't sit still. I liked to apply myself to as many things as possible—jazz band, debating team, art projects, volleyball team, school musicals, magicians' club, orienteering, coaching the hockey team, school orchestra. You name it, I probably did it. So much so that at the end of primary school, I was voted the person most likely to squeeze twenty-five hours into a day.

But this wasn't a very cool thing for a high school student. As I entered into the world of secondary education, I was hit with a confronting reality: I was out of the safety of a nurturing primary school a few blocks away from our family home, and I was beginning to step out into the world on my own.

As a family living on two teachers' salaries*, we didn't live a lavish lifestyle. Mum and Dad always provided everything we needed to have the best education possible, but sacrifices were made to make this happen. When I wanted to start learning the saxophone, or take up hockey, or perform in the school musical, Dad took on a second job; our holidays were always a fun but affordable affair. So when I received a full academic scholarship for a local private high school, I'm sure this would have been a

---

* Teachers are drastically underpaid for the impact they have and the hours they have to put in. Throughout 2022 teachers were repetitively on strike over ongoing salary disputes. The pay is so low that there are nowhere near enough people who want to train as teachers and many classrooms across the country are full of students with no teachers to teach them.

great relief to my parents to have all of my school fees covered for the duration of my secondary education.

Being a bit of an overachiever, I was used to copping a bit of bullying throughout primary school. The 'tall poppy syndrome' is rife in Australia. As a society, we are eager to back the underdog, but those who dare to rise above the average are quickly cut down to size. It was perhaps because it is such a pivotal time for young teenagers who are forming their identity, but I was the butt of many jokes. Making others laugh at the expense of another seemed to be pretty common amongst twelve- and thirteen-year-olds. And it turned out that I was an easy target.

So as a kid, I had developed a number of coping strategies to try and not let the bullying affect me. But I wasn't prepared for the level of ostracism at high school. I tried everything to fix the problem. With much support from a private counsellor and my Mum in particular doing all she could to help me try to deal with these school-yard challenges, I tried every strategy from ignoring to confronting and everything in between, but nothing worked. So, in the end, we decided I needed to move schools. And to my parents credit, even though I would lose the financial benefit of my scholarship, they supported me all the way.

The next week we signed up for tours at a list of new schools and began the task of finding a new high school for the second time in twelve months. When I walked into the last school on our list, I knew I had found the right place for me. I entered the music centre and my eyes widened at the sight of the large framed photographs of the annual school musicals lining the hallways. Room after room was full of music lessons in progress and the grand sound of a classical melody carried down the corridor from the orchestra in rehearsal. The art centre was an explosion of colour, modelling clay, paintings, sculptures and student artwork everywhere. And then I walked into the media centre and my eyes widened further still. An iconic 'recording' sign flashed overhead a door that led into a film studio full of TV cameras, film sets and studio lights. Off to the side, students were producing an actual TV show from the studio control room while other students were hiring film equipment for their projects or editing films in a room lined with computers.

I was home. There wasn't something wrong with me at my old school, I was just in the wrong place. I settled in quickly at my new school and soon found a group of like-minded friends who weren't critical of those who were ambitious and applied themselves, but instead revelled in it.

In the second year at my new school, the entire cohort of Year 10's were instructed that we would be creating a 'Personal Project': a nine-month assignment to produce something self-led that we were passionate about. It could be anything from restoring a couch or volunteering with a charity to building a model aeroplane or composing a piece of music.

I knew immediately what I was going to do—I wanted to express the impact that bullying had had on me. Everyone knew that bullying was bad, but I hadn't ever heard any stories from people who had actually been bullied. At the time I was big fan of Aardman's 'Wallace and Grommit' stop-motion animations, so I thought telling this story as a claymation could be fun.

With nine months to create my piece, I set about to produce my first stop-motion film. I immersed myself in writing the story, building the miniature sets and constructing the characters from plasticine. Needless to say, creating a film by taking a single photograph, moving the character a tiny amount, and taking another photo is very time consuming. On average, I would animate between three to six hours each afternoon when I got home from school and would finish the night with about five seconds of film to show for it.

After I had completed a few scenes, the Head of Media heard about what I was working on and was instantly excited about my project and strongly encouraged my passion. I had learnt from my own parents that teachers love passionate students, so I was more than grateful to take up his support. He let me borrow some film lights and set up my animation studio in a corner of a work room to animate each scene. Mum and Dad were grateful to get their sunroom back and all of the desk lamps from across the house were returned to their rightful tables.

The story for my film was to be inspired by my own experiences: a young boy called 'Larry' who doesn't fit in with the other kids and has subsequently become a bit of a loner at school. A couple of bigger kids make fun of him, calling him names when he's left out of a basketball game. He goes home with a big tin of grey paint, a roller in hand, and he covers over everything in his room, blocking out the world. All looks lost until the kindness of just one person makes him realises that someone cares about him.

It was not a particularly long film, running at seven minutes, capturing five seconds of film a day, but it took the full nine months to finish it. Friends and teachers lent their voices for the soundtrack, I edited the film with music and titles and the Media Assistant gave me a crash course in Photoshop so I could design the VHS video cover. And so my first ever film, creatively titled *Larry*, was completed.

For a bit of fun, we held a film premiere in our lounge room at home and invited all of my friends and teachers who had helped to come and view it. Dad even set up two folding directors' chairs up front for the Head of Media and the Media Assistant to take VIP positions. Everybody crammed into our house for the big event and because the film was so short, we had to play it a couple of times to make the night worthwhile. For a first film made by a fifteen-year-old, it's an ambitious and impressive piece, full of heart and a story that can be understood regardless of language. Even now I enjoy watching it, at least until it gets to the credits where it reads like an egotistical org chart: Written by Henry Smith, Directed by Henry Smith, Character Design by Henry Smith, Music by Henry Smith, Sound Design by Henry Smith, Catering by Henry Smith*. If nothing else, this proved the point that I needed to find some other filmmakers to start working with.

---

* Gotta credit yourself for feeding yourself, right?

Of course, in a room of friends and family, everyone was extremely supportive. But to my great surprise, in the weeks that followed, after I'd entered it into a number of film festivals around the world, not only did it get accepted and screened, but it started winning. 'Best Animation', 'Audience Choice', 'Best of the Festival'. I was blown away. I'm pretty sure it wasn't the quality of the filmmaking that people were connecting with, but the story. People were resonating with a story that they could relate to.

By this point, there was no going back. I had firmly fallen in love with filmmaking. But more than that, I had found purpose. Or rather, purpose had found me.

Purpose is something that goes beyond ourselves. For me, I had fallen in love with telling stories that nourish and inspire people. It's not about how many awards the film won, or even how many people saw it, but how many people it affected. I loved seeing the impact my little animation had, its ability to comfort and console people, to teach and empower. *Larry* went on to become an educational resource used in schools across the country to encourage kids to talk about bullying and the negative effect of harassment. I discovered that stories, whether told through a film or spoken around a campfire, are an incredibly powerful way to deeply connect with people.

Over fifteen years later, I visited one of Australia's top commercial film production companies to meet with the founder. I was interested to learn about their success and hear their story of how they got there. From the outset, everything was intimidatingly impressive (most likely intentional I'm guessing). A super fancy building with futuristic meeting pods and a gleaming motorbike in the front reception, a disproportionately high number of very good-looking staff and various production departments working on all gamut of creative things from TV commercials and feature films to augmented reality and tech development. They were developing a monstrous amount of very high-quality (and high-budget!) content each year, and had a wall of shelves groaning under the weight of countless awards to prove it. On our tour, the founder took me through all of the impressive facilities and made sure that we walked down through the basement to admire her Porsche in the carpark. Like the shiny surface of the sports car, everything reflected success, but something niggled at me. It all felt a little empty.

When we sat down and spoke, it became evident very quickly that she was bored and lost in life. She was at the peak of her career, had all the awards and acclaim, and had become very wealthy in the process. But what motivates you to get out of bed once you've reached your goal and achieved all that you want for yourself? She had even tried to remedy the situation by funding various charitable initiatives within the company, but she was empty.

She didn't have purpose. Which meant that she didn't have a compelling reason to get up and tackle each day. And no matter how much 'stuff' you add to your life to keep busy, if there's no purpose at the centre, the spark soon flickers and dies. Purpose is the engine at the centre that drives everything we do. It's what drives every action and motivates every decision.

When I found my purpose at fifteen, it became my engine. Everything I did was powered by this reason and became my motivation to give everything I had.

TAKEAWAYS

Purpose is the engine. Purpose is the motivation to get out of bed every day, knowing that we are working towards something truly meaningful.

CHAPTER TWO | **PERSONAL PURPOSE**

Your Purpose Is Bigger Than You

While devastating and extremely challenging for so many, Covid-19 did a spectacular job at shining a spotlight on purpose. The Great Pause gave us all a once-in-a-lifetime opportunity to reassess what's important in life.

I had drafted up a plan to shift to remote work back in 2019. When the pandemic started, I was one year into a five-year scheme to work from home starting with one day a week, increasing a day each year. My wife and I were inching our life towards a plan to be able to move out of a busy city lifestyle and to enjoy a more balanced life raising a family in a spacious (and more affordable!) regional area, while still being able to operate as film producers and directors. Thanks to Covid, we were able to fast-track our plans. One week into the pandemic, we all switched to working remotely and, within a month, we had seized the opportunity, packed up our inner-city home and moved out ninety minutes to the gorgeous Blue Mountains.

Almost overnight, everyone that we worked with had become a Zoom native, accustomed to operating almost entirely remotely and had quickly become comfortable with not needing to be in the same room to operate effectively. It took a global pandemic to implement a one hundred percent user uptake of this new way of thinking and working, without which remote working would have always struggled to take off.

This new opportunity gave us all many opportunities to stop and reassess. We've questioned why we should spend hours in traffic commuting to an office every day when many professions have proved work can be done remotely. Why must we work restricting hours that mean we miss out on the school drop-off and pick-up for our kids? Why are we working for a company that isn't doing anything to make the world a better place? Why do we do what we do? To answer this question with certainty, we have to know what our purpose is in life.

Firstly, purpose isn't to be mistaken with goals. We should all have aspiring goals in life—to be drafted for a professional basketball team, to get signed by a major record label, to be the CEO of a multinational tech company, to be a great stay-at-home parent to your children. These are all great goals: they are measurable, time-based and/or actionable.

Perhaps, if you're like me, you may have struggled to set proper goals. At the start of each year, I would get super-motivated to set myself up for a great year and to achieve more than I did the past year. And so I would set goals to help me keep focussed, increase our revenue by twenty percent, serve a higher number of customers, donate a certain amount to charity, grow our team by twenty-five percent. But after a few months I would lose motivation. Besides achievement for achievement's sake, why was I pursuing these goals?

Super simple answer: they weren't linked to my purpose.

Purpose is bigger than our goals. Purpose is out of reach. Unobtainable. When you're aligned to your purpose, it's the thing that motivates you to get up every day and gets you excited to take on the world. Goals naturally emerge as we work out how to move further and further into our purpose. As motivational author Simon Sinek says, it's your 'why'.

So how do you find your purpose?

I'll give you a clue: if you're focussing entirely on yourself to try and find your purpose, you won't.

When I was a kid, I was obsessed with building treehouses. Not playing in them, just the building. Every day during the school holidays, I would be outside up in a tree creating another imaginative leafy fort. Finding great spots in trees, working out how I would construct the framework up in the branches, foraging for bits of old timber from Dad's shed, rigging up retractable ladders on pulley systems and a variety of trap doors to keep people out. I loved it!*

But after I would finish building the treehouse, the joy of creating had finished and I would quickly lose interest. It was fun to play in when friends came over, but then they'd go home

---

* As I'm sure you can imagine, the 1960s film *Swiss Family Robinson* was an absolute childhood favourite. I spent hours and hours poring over their incredible treehouse constructions—I couldn't get enough of it. That was until I rewatched it as an adult and discovered the crazy amount of animal cruelty. Don't worry, I didn't take any inspiration from those parts!

and I had no real desire to play in it. So I'd move on to building another treehouse. And then another, and another, until I ran out of trees. I found a lot of joy in the creating part because my mind was active and I was solving problems, but as soon as I stopped, I'd become bored, restless and unsatisfied. I'd achieved my goal but there was a part of me that wanted more.

I was lucky to have an aunty who shared my love of building adventurous constructions. She delighted in spending time with me and my cousins and, as a teacher of people living with disability, she took great joy in involving us in activities that she knew would challenge us. So helping her to build a chook house, constructing wooden treasure boxes, crafting percussive musical instruments and making forts out of sheets and blankets were part of a usual day at her house.

One summer she noticed that since moving out to the country, my youngest cousin Louis didn't have a treehouse of his own. He had loved playing in mine when he'd come to visit, but was a bit too young to build his own. So during the holidays we travelled for hours out of Adelaide to Louis's house to build him a treehouse. In a magnificent white cedar in his backyard, Aunty Lisa and I created a masterful treehouse with a retractable ladder, a braided rope railing, a handy weather station and a wicker basket on a pulley for hoisting up goodies. She brought all of her power tools and a trailer full of timber so I was in my element.

Like each of the times I had built my own treehouses back at home, building one for Louis had filled me with great joy. But this time it felt different. Once we finished building it, Louis was delighted to play in it. He ran up and down the ladder, checked all of the instruments on his weather station, shouted something about pirates over the railing and pulled up his pet rabbit in the basket. This time I felt a new sense of satisfaction. Not from the creating part, but by creating something that brought joy to another person. Years later, I realised that in this moment, I had uncovered another part of my own purpose.

Purpose is bigger than you. At its simplest level, your purpose is beneficial to somebody else.

So back to you—how do you discover what your purpose is? Luckily, it's easy to work out because you know it deep down already. Most likely it's just not something you focus on regularly. Adam Leipzig, an American film and theatre producer, gave an excellent TED talk on how to find your purpose which articulates this beautifully*.

---

* 'How to know your life purpose in 5 minutes': www.youtube.com/watch?v=vVsXO9brK7M&t

It's well worth a watch, but here's the top-line. Your purpose will articulate these questions:

1. Who are you?
2. What do you do?
3. Who do you do it for?
4. How does it help them?
5. How are they changed as a consequence?

Notice that the majority of these points are about others, not yourself. Your purpose is for the benefit of others. So for me, here's how it looks:

1. Who are you?
   HENRY

2. What do you do?
   I AM A STORYTELLER

3. Who do you do it for?
   EVERYONE!

4. How does it help them?
   IT BRINGS JOY, MOTIVATION + HOPE

5. How are they changed as a consequence?
   PEOPLE ARE NOURISHED + INSPIRED

So here's my purpose: My name is Henry and I create things that inspire and nourish people.

My purpose brings joy to other people. When I am fully operating in my purpose, by default it benefits others. But don't worry—you absolutely get the benefit too. When you know your purpose and operate in it, going after it each day feels good. Not just as a figure of speech, but biologically your body automatically initiates a threefold chemical reaction that makes you feel on top of the world.

Firstly, pursuing your purpose and contributing to someone else's happiness unlocks serotonin (the 'happiness drug') throughout your own body. Secondly, as you are figuring out how to get there, dopamine (the 'problem-solving drug') is released and courses through your veins, increasing your ability to think and plan. And then once you succeed and make others happy, oxytocin (the 'love drug') is unlocked and fills your body. In short—fulfilling your purpose actually makes you feel good!

TAKEAWAYS

Purpose is bigger than your goals. Goals naturally emerge when we begin to move towards our purpose, and are just steps to help us get closer.

Purpose is bigger than you. Our purpose is for the benefit of others.

Purpose makes you feel good. Seriously. When we operate in our purpose, our bodies biologically react to unlock serotonin, dopamine and oxytocin.

CHAPTER THREE | PURPOSE VS PROFIT

Purpose Isn't a Slap of Paint on the Outside

Organisations exist with profit or purpose at the centre of their existence. Not both.

Don't be fooled by what their marketing might have you believe—an organisation is either driven by profit or it is driven by purpose. One is in conflict with the other, so anyone that tells you they are led by both is only deceiving themselves. An organisation can absolutely be purpose-led and make a profit, or profit-led and have purpose, but it can only be driven at its core by one or the other.

Profit-led versus purpose-led. What's the difference?

To be profit-led is to exist first and foremost to make money. This is the situation for most companies in existence today, predominantly because this is why you start a business, or it is what the shareholders demand: to make money. Profit-led companies survive by profiting off others, whether an individual, a community or the environment. An energy drink manufacturer selling sugary, caffeinated drinks, knowing full well that their product gives no long-term nutritional value to the consumer. Fashion brands that have young people believing that they will look beautiful or desirable if they wear their garments. Tech moguls presenting social media apps under the guise of community-building platforms when in reality they are deliberately developed to be highly addictive, difficult to leave and result in high levels of depression, anxiety and social phobias. Need I go on?

On the other end of the seesaw, purpose-led is to be driven by a purpose that gives a positive value to a person/group/environment, subsequently solving a problem. A company selling toilet paper to fund sanitation projects in developing countries, a film school educating young adults with disabilities to gain professional creative employment, or a social enterprise that sells consumer products to reduce extreme poverty.

This important differentiator determines everything within the organisation and culminates in either a 'push' or 'pull' mentality. People are either pushed to do what an organisation wants them to do, or they are naturally pulled towards what the organisation is doing because they are being offered something that genuinely benefits them.

Purpose is the engine on the inside, not a slap of paint on the outside. So to retrofit a profit-led company to be purpose-led requires a top to bottom restart, starting with purpose. And there's a lot of companies that try to do this, and quickly realise that to do it properly is no quick change!

Let's look a little deeper at what makes a company profit-led or purpose-led ...

Profit-led

Profit-led companies, companies with a push mentality, are always pushing people (both workers and consumers) to get the company's desired outcomes. Why the need to push? Because there's no motivation for staff or consumers to help a company to make money. This model is the norm across the world. In fact, this push mentality is so ingrained into society that we barely register this as a problem anymore.

The four-step formula behind this profit-led mentality is common and simple:
1. Profit
2. Channels
3. Product
4. Value

At the very beginning, you start a company with the fundamental intention to generate wealth (profit). So you start with the question, 'How can I make money?'. It's a logical reason why many companies start. The next question is then, 'Who can I make money from?' Who would be willing to pay for something (channels)?

Once you have the channels, you need something to sell to these people in order to make money from them (product). What product or service can you sell? You could wash windows, bake cookies, do people's taxes, advise on interior decorating, design children's shoes, or babysit exotic animals*.

Now all you need to do is to articulate the value of what you have to sell so people will buy it and you can make money from them.

It begins with the need to make money, and what value it actually brings to the individual/community/environment comes last. It's fair to say that plenty of people start with a need. They come across an individual or group who need a solution to something. But, at the end of the day, what is the long-term motivation? Is it, first and foremost, to solve the need, or is the need an opportunity to make money? When the need to make money is the founding driver, it can be difficult to articulate its value to others, as the original intent wasn't about adding value to them—it was to make money from them.

---

* Not an exclusive list but by all means feel free to take up exotic animal babysitting.

Purpose-led

Purpose-led organisations are not just different, but the complete opposite of this. When someone or something is purpose-led, people can't help but to be pulled towards that. The reason is that the formula is flipped:

1. Value
2. Product
3. Channels
4. Profit

You start with the need to give value to another that solves a problem (value). In 2006, Blake Mycoskie saw the hardships faced by children without shoes. In 2009, my lovely wife Genevieve met a young aspiring actor with Down syndrome who had been told he'd never get the opportunity to perform. Both very clear problems that need solutions.

With the motivation to deliver value locked in the crosshairs, you then set out trying to find a way to deliver that value (product). Blake started a shoe company called TOMS which committed that for every pair of shoes sold, they would donate a pair of shoes to a child in need. Genevieve started

Bus Stop Films as an inclusive film school to offer pathways into the film industry for people with disabilities.*

Then you need to create opportunities for people to experience or engage with the product (channels). Start an online store, run film classes in the local community centre— anything to reach people.

Then lastly you get to profit; you need to find a way to make the business model viable. There's no point starting an amazing company that solves an important problem if it runs out of money and can't afford to stay open. There is nothing wrong with making profit, in fact it's very important. I'm a big fan of the term 'profit for purpose'—generating profit to do good.

But when profit is the initial driver, it will always be a case of 'my will over yours'. Leadership is the same. A leader's drive and leadership style can be either profit-led or purpose-led.

---

* More on this amazing story in Chapter Seven.

Purpose-led leadership

In 2011, I was travelling around Australia filming a project at a conference for high school leaders where they were sharing their ideas to change the world for the better. The level of thinking coming from these school kids was incredibly inspiring. Their ideas ranged from creating teenage-relevant news sources and eradicating discrimination to curing loneliness, alleviating the pressures of mental illness, exposing the damage of drinking culture, and the individual and community benefits of social acceptance.

In between filming, I was fortunate enough to hear one of the keynote speakers: an extremely passionate, purpose-led business leader sharing his story of their social enterprise. Daniel Flynn had founded Thankyou with his then girlfriend (now wife) in a bid to help end extreme poverty. Here was a business that had flipped the formula and was now getting the attention of many around the world. It was birthed out of creating actual value for individuals and communities and had worked outwards from that position.

A couple of years later I was honoured to be able to produce and direct a film for one of their major fundraising campaigns.

The campaign was an ambitious venture to raise $1.2 million in thirty days through the sale of Daniel's 'pay what you want' priced book to fund their next step in world-changing growth. The film was relatively simple on paper: a seven-and-a-half-minute single-take film of Daniel walking through a warehouse, talking to camera and inviting viewers to join the cause and explaining how it would all work. Logistically, of course, it was a little more challenging with moving sets, a cast of many (including a number of babies and children), time pressures, a very small film crew, and Daniel's unwavering commitment to memorise the script and deliver it without a teleprompter in one go.

The end result was a very effective film that went on to help Thankyou raise $2.5 million and fast-track Daniel as a best-selling author. Many have asked how we pulled off such an effective result, but the answer has always been very simple—when an organisation is not led by profit but is truly led by purpose, everything else flows smoothly. We didn't need any advertising trickery to manipulate the viewer in any way and push them to do what we wanted. We just needed to create the platform to let Thankyou share the product that delivers the problem-solving value.

When it comes to leadership, leaders are either profit-led or purpose-led. Profit-led leadership functions to profit from others (my will over yours) whereas purpose-led leadership is grounded in serving others (how can I help you). This certainly isn't to say that you shouldn't make a profit—a by-product of purpose-led leadership can certainly be making money—but first and foremost, purpose-led leaders exist to serve.

To lead with purpose is the combination of knowing three things:
1. Who you are there to serve
2. Your solution to their problem
3. Your natural talent.

Purpose-led leaders know who they are there to help: a neighbourhood of elderly people, a network of small business leaders, young men suffering from depression, first-time mums. And, of course, a problem that this group of people share: no access to clean drinking water, the challenge of employing values-aligned staff, an inability to finance a home loan, the struggle to get out of bed each morning. No matter how large or small, it is a problem that is waiting to be solved.

Secondly, purpose-led leaders are driven by finding a solution to this problem. Not just the fix, but the why behind their solution. Simon Sinek famously teaches about starting with the why and this is absolutely true*. Why are you trying to solve, or at least reduce this problem? Knowing and understanding our 'why' becomes the driving force when we inevitably get tired. The 'why' will motivate us each morning and remind us to take our eyes off ourselves and our circumstances, and to look to those who need our solution.

And lastly, a purpose-led leader has a unique asset that they bring to the table—a natural talent. There are countless problems to be solved in the world, but when we can solve a problem by using a natural talent that we possess, things really start to move. Whether it be baking cakes, financial management, writing books for children, motivating people or, in my case, storytelling, when we use our talent to solve a problem this creates the authenticity that will surpass the times we hit pushback, criticism, roadblocks and dead ends.

---

* Sinek's books, *Start With Why* and *Find Your Why* are a great place to start. Or just watch his Ted Talk if you're in a hurry.

TAKEAWAYS

Organisations can only serve one master; profit or purpose. A profit-led business cannot have true purpose, however a purpose-led business can make profit.

Profit-led businesses #1 function is to generate wealth for its shareholders. They must operate in a push mentality to achieved its desired outcomes.

Purpose-led businesses #1 function is to give positive value to a person/group/environment. People can't help but to be pulled into their orbit.

A purpose-led leader knows where they are going. They understand who they are serving, their solution to the problem and the natural talent that they bring to the table.

47

PART TWO

Purposeful Life

CHAPTER FOUR | COURAGE

My Best Friend Gave Me the Greatest Give of All

Our purpose is for the benefit of other people. When we are operating in our purpose, countless others are better off for it. I learnt this first-hand from my childhood best mate.

The first time I saw him, I didn't like the look of him at all. I was 12 and I had walked up the road to our church. The church minister had recently accepted a new job elsewhere and so a new minister had just moved into the manse next to the church. And with him came his family, including two sons: Chris and his younger brother, Michael. As I walked towards the church past the car park, I spotted the two new residents playing basketball. But Chris wasn't just shooting some casual hoops; he had all the gear: the sunnies, basketball shoes and matching sweatbands on his head and wrists. While I was an active kid, I was not really a sporty kid. I just knew Chris and I wouldn't get along.

But how wrong I was.

Chris seemed to be passionate about everything. Cricket, cooking, drama classes, playing the drums, ska music, even competitive tenpin bowling. And not just a little bit interested, but passionate. He threw himself headfirst into everything. But what he was most passionate about was people. Talking to him, you knew you had his full attention and he was genuinely interested in what you had to say.

We quickly bonded. I had found someone who liked to pursue their passions as much as I did, and someone who got excited if I was excited about something. We both loved to cook so we signed ourselves up to be the cooks for the church youth camp, complete with matching homemade chef's pants. We both loved percussion instruments, so we attended African drum workshops and built our own instruments to play in the church band.

One afternoon after school, I sat at the piano at Chris's house and taught him the words of an Irish children's song called 'Ma, ma, will you buy me'. Written from the perspective of an overly needy child, it's one of those tedious kids songs with endlessly repetitive lyrics. First he wants his mum to buy him a banana. Then he needs her help to peel the banana. Then he asks her to take a bite. Then he gets upset that she ate too much. So then he wants her to buy him a new banana. And back to the start of the song we go.

It's infuriating to listen to for more than a minute because it just never finishes. So naturally Chris and I delighted in playing endless rounds until after everyone in Chris's family had escaped behind closed doors. By our thirtieth round, we thought we were quite clever when we substituted other fruit into our lyrics, but apparently even this streak of creative brilliance wasn't enough to save our performance. Eventually Chris's mum cleverly coaxed us away from the piano with the lure of ice blocks outside.

A few weeks later I saw a news report about sick kids in hospital who were battling awful illnesses and diseases and how a group of performers had dressed up as 'clown doctors' to put a smile on their faces. Dressed in white lab coats but with pockets overflowing with oversized bicycle horns, furry puppets, novelty medical equipment, balloon animals, and each of them donning a matching red nose, the clown doctors brought so much joy and hope to the kids and their parents. Not only had they helped to brighten up the entire ward, but it was medically proven that these visits were fast-tracking the kids' healing journeys. I was immediately hooked by this and then, of course, so too was Chris.

So, without delay, Chris and I began creating our own clown costumes and choreographed routines that would make people smile. Chris found a brightly coloured suit at an op shop and I pinched a pair of green and white striped overalls from my aunty as well as my sister's long rainbow socks. We borrowed my dad's old wheelbarrow, fastened a rainbow umbrella atop and filled it to the brim with beach buckets full of confetti, musical instruments, hidden compartments loaded with coloured scarves and an assortment of magic tricks. Attributed to our new clown wigs—mine a rainbow afro and Chris's a shaggy rainbow hairdo—'Mullet and Fluff' were born.

We performed at kids' birthday parties, youth group camps and church productions and appeared in our local Christmas pageant on numerous occasions. I had been a naturally shy and hesitant kid but, with Chris around, I felt like I could do anything. He had the ability to know when I was doubting a decision and he could fill me with courage. Chris would look straight at me and say, 'You can do it.'

Once we became teenagers, we were set to start at different high schools. At his house one day after school, I was telling him about an opportunity at my new school. The music department had lots of bands and there was an opening to play piano in the school's top jazz band. Being in Year 9 and new to the school, I felt I was way too young for the position. This band competed in national competitions around the country and all of the other students were two to three years older than me.

But of course, Chris looked at me and said, 'You can do it.'

The word encourage literally means 'to put courage into'. From the Latin 'encorage', 'en' is to 'put into' plus 'corage' is 'courage' or 'heart'. Chris would literally put courage into me.

I auditioned the next day and was soon after offered the role, becoming the youngest member of the band.

Together, Chris and I even managed to get jobs as kitchen hands at a local conference centre. We would spend hours telling stories, making up songs and cracking jokes while we worked until eventually the management stopped scheduling us on the same shifts. I think they thought that we weren't working as hard just because we were having fun.

But it was all cut short.

When he was just 17, Chris received news that he had an aggressive form of leukaemia and would need to start treatment straight away. No more cooking, no more cricket and no more bowling. No more drama club, no more drums and no more clowning. He immediately went into treatment and spent the next two years in and out of hospital, fighting the disease incredibly hard.

As Chris spent many long months in hospital, completely depleted by the ferocity of the medication, there were no clown doctors who came to cheer him up. His hair had fallen out, his face had swollen from the treatment and he had just enough energy to hold short conversations with his family and visitors.

Chris died six months after his bone marrow transplant. On the morning of his death, to the surprise of his family he had sat upright in bed and burst into a round of 'Ma, ma, will you buy me'. While he couldn't sustain the usual fifty-something rounds of lyrics, his weak voice filled his room with joy, delighting his family who sat by his bedside. Chris didn't need to wait for a clown doctor to cheer up the room. Even with the last breaths in his body, he was devoted to imparting life into everyone around him.

His death was felt deeply through our whole community and left many people searching for answers, trying to understand how this could happen. He was dearly loved by so many and his passion for life had impacted hundreds of people. His funeral filled the entire church, overflowing to the hall next door and out into the corridors.

I won't ever know why Chris got that disease, how come he couldn't beat it or why the life of someone so young ended like that. He was so full of life and had so much promise for his future. But I was the luckiest person to be able to spend my teenage years with someone who filled me with so much courage. And when it came from someone like Chris, that courage doesn't dim inside of you easily.

TAKEAWAYS

Passionate curiosity in other people shows that you are genuinely interested in them as a person.

Encouragement is powerful. To encourage someone is literally to put courage into them.

CHAPTER FIVE | **A START**
Create a Space Just Your Size

Creating my stop-motion film *Larry*, I had uncovered a purpose that made me really excited. I wanted to chase that feeling of making movies and telling stories that made people feel good. I had made *Larry* pretty much all by myself in the corner of a room and taught myself a lot of what I needed to know. But that was only going to get me so far ... I needed to take the next step and learn from more experienced storytellers and filmmakers.

At this time in the early 2000s, a staple of the Australian television line-up was filming just an hour out of Adelaide. Set on the fictional Drover's Run in outback Australia, *McLeod's Daughters* was one of the first TV series to feature rural Australian women as the main protagonists. In South Australia we didn't have a very big film industry, so eight seasons of production meant steady employment for the state's best filmmakers.

I had selected very specific film festivals to enter *Larry*, namely festivals that had a free or low entry fee. Very fortunately for me, a gentleman called Tony Cronin had gone along to one of these festivals to watch the closing night and had seen my film. As well as being a lover of film, Tony was the production designer for *McLeod's Daughters*. I can't remember why, but for some reason I wasn't able to be at the festival's closing event, so Mum and Dad had gone along in my place. When my little stop-motion film won the top gong of the whole festival, Tony was keen to pass on his congratulations so naturally he got stuck talking to my very proud parents.

Tony must have seen something in that film because he offered me work experience with him on the film set for later that year. I could hardly believe it when my parents relayed the story to me that evening.

When I arrived very early to the film set some six weeks later, I had big stars in my eyes. Despite it being the early days of the internet, I had scoured every video and book I could get my hands on to learn as much as I could about the magic of filmmaking. This was nothing like my stop-motion film set on *Larry*. Where I had used my desk lamp and a second-hand photography lamp, here there were trucks full of ginormous lights that were rigged to shine like sunlight through windows. Where I had built a camera slider from two metal poles and a long threaded crank to move my $700 Handycam, here there were large film cameras being operated by people on cranes that hoisted them and the cameras high up into the sky. I was met by a self-sufficient village of crew, equipment, power generators, hair and makeup trucks, specialty vehicles and a huge marquee with rows of chairs and tables laden with food for the cast and crew. Film sets are often described as the circus coming to town, and it absolutely was. They had everything they needed to be completely self-contained out in rural Australia.

I spent two thrilling weeks working with Tony and his art department doing any odd jobs they needed. The series was shot on a 150-year-old homestead so there was plenty for us to do to ensure that it looked like a working farm. We part-built new fences to look like the actors were constructing them, we stuck fake signage on the side of trucks and utes, we made roast chickens for a dinner party, we added dust to old photo frames and moved around plenty of furniture. I was infatuated by all of the magic—a secret gas line ran into the dining room fireplace that meant they could turn the fire on and off at will from the room next door, the makeup department would apply a veneer of dirt and sweat so the actors looked as though they had been working outside all day, a fire bellow filled with dust allowed the art department to make a stationary car look like it had just screeched into the driveway with instant dust clouds. There was a hidden room in the homestead with walls covered in soundproofing eggshell foam and hessian sacks for the actors to record lines of dialogue that would be later edited into a scene. I was as happy as a kid in a candy shop.

As we drew near the end of my second week on set, Tony sat me down for a bit of career advice. 'So what do you think?' he asked. 'See a role that you want to do in the future?' Judging by the *Larry* credit roll where I had listed myself in every role from animation and sound recordist to set design and catering, this was a fair question. Thinking Tony could be my ticket into the film industry, I told him that I really liked the art department and could see a future as a production designer. But he'd seen how I'd longingly watched the camera department and had deduced that the area I was really interested in was cinematography. 'You can't get halfway up the production design ladder, and expect to step across into the camera department at the same level,' Tony informed me. 'You start back at the bottom. You need to think about which ladder you want to get to the top of, and start climbing that one.'

So that lunchtime, Tony pointed out the esteemed Roger Dowling ACS to me. As the Director of Photography, Roger stood at the top of the camera department ladder. He was a kind and softly-spoken man, but I was shaking with nerves. With Tony's wise words in mind, I timidly asked to sit with him as he finished his lunch and managed to fumble my way through a list of questions I had been dying to ask him. Roger was, of course, very encouraging and spent the rest of his lunch break answering questions and giving advice on how to get started as a cinematographer.

I had found the right ladder and was keen to start climbing.

As I entered into my final year of high school, I was confronted by how much the schooling system is tailored to a certain type of learning and a certain type of person. I saw many other talented students think that they weren't smart enough, just because they didn't fit into the system very well. I happened to be one of the lucky ones. I loved to learn and I thrived in an academic environment that had a clear grading system to determine success. My innate desire to please people and do the right thing was well suited to thrive in this type of environment.

So it's probably no surprise that I was excited at the prospect of going to university. Growing up with two teachers as parents, I had heard wonderful stories from their time at university and the importance of good education—the prestige of the grand sandstone buildings, the welcome challenge of a higher level of study and newly-found independence of navigating life as a young adult. I had high expectations and couldn't wait to start.

Unfortunately for me, South Australia isn't known for its tertiary film programs and, up to this point, I hadn't really considered the possibilities of studying interstate or further abroad. When I examined the local options available to me, the top course boasted having taught many of South Australia's most notable filmmakers. I figured that if it was good enough for them, surely it would be good enough for me.

Out of a maximum Tertiary Entrance Rank (TER) score of 100, graduating high school students must achieve at least 60.0 to be allowed admission to this course. Friends around me were looking into courses with a high score entry of 90.0 or 95.0, so the bar for my course was certainly not high and it definitely didn't excite me. I had always taken the path less travelled and I wanted to study in a course that would challenge me. But what this process did do was motivate me to set my own challenge as I entered into Year 12: if I only needed a TER score of 60.0, I wondered what was the highest that I could achieve.

This became fundamental to having a fantastic last year at high school. As most of my friends became increasingly stressed with mounting assignments and exam pressure, I was instead excited because I didn't have the pressure of my career goals attached to a number. I was already very focussed and attentive in all of my subjects, but in my final year I pushed even harder. I put every effort into each task and assignment, crammed for exams and dared to think outside the box for my projects. I even signed up for extra classes and took on leadership roles. An absolute overachiever, I was comfortable in the knowledge that I would likely achieve the 60.0 minimum entry, so I gave myself permission to loosen up a little, make space to try different things and enjoy my final year of schooling in a way that I probably would have normally avoided.

I finished the year with a score of 98.7, earning the principal's school award and enough eye-rolls from my friends to last a lifetime. But I was proud of what I'd achieved. Not only had I pushed myself as far as I could, but I had enjoyed the process and was ready to launch into university. So in 2007 I began the next chapter of my exciting adventure.

Except it wasn't exciting.

The university film studies program I had been accepted into may have been the best in the state, but it was entry level. And despite having just completed three years of film and media studies in high school, prior learning wasn't accepted so I couldn't just jump ahead a year or two. There was nothing fundamentally wrong with the course, I just got bored way too quickly and so I struggled to sit still.

Back when I was seven, my parents got me tested for attention deficit disorder (ADD). I had been getting bored in class at primary school and it was showing. I would finish my work too quickly and run out of things to do. I couldn't figure out why the other kids still had all their heads down. Luckily, I had a very cluey Year 2 teacher who sat my parents down and said, 'Henry's either naughty or smart. And I don't think he's naughty.'

So, some ten years later, sitting through an entry-level film course was a recipe for disaster. I had suspected that I may not be challenged by the course but I had high hopes of meeting other filmmakers and making great films together as a team*.

Unfortunately, physically making films was quite a way off in their filmmaking curriculum. First, we had to sit through a lot of theory, pass basic equipment-handling tests to prove our competency, and create production design collages from old lifestyle magazines. Excited to finally be able to use a camera, I over-exerted myself in a simple cinematography assignment

---

* Remembering I had proudly listed myself in every role on the crew for *Larry*, I was keen to change and learn how to work with other filmmakers.

and was failed for not fulfilling the brief. At the end of a term dedicated to an introduction to camera framing, we were instructed to simply demonstrate our understanding of camera shot sizes by filming a list of shots one after another on a DV Cam without editing. But having seen the opportunity to finally create something, I ended up over-producing the assignment by working in a narrative, character development, titles, visual effects and a soundtrack. The lecturer seemed bemused by my response to the basic assignment, but ultimately had to fail me for not executing the instructions properly.

But the shining light was that we could volunteer on the film projects of older students. I immediately put my hand up for every role I could. I did the catering for a backyard suburban drama (I recruited my Grandma to make hundreds of scones with me), I produced a short film about modern-day vampires, and I volunteered in the camera department for a 1960s-style Italian action-adventure parody series*.

But between these projects I was getting bored. I had kept in touch with Tony Cronin so I began pestering him to see if I

---

* This actually went on to become very successful, with a TV-series spin off funded years later. YouTube *Italian Spiderman Trailer* for a great laugh.

could get any voluntary work on the projects he was working on. After months of my polite but persistent chasing, Tony got me an interview with a producer of a short film that was about to shoot for five days up the coast. I was so hungry for a challenge that I was happy to work for free and take on any role I could to chase my dream of working in the camera department. I landed the gig as a camera attachment (a trainee camera assistant), informed my lecturers I would be missing a few classes and packed my bags.

As soon as I was on set, I was happy again. I loved the order and the professionalism of a film set, the way people spoke to each other, the camaraderie of solving problems under pressure and being part of a team that was creating something magical. And best of all, I got to meet other producers who were working on upcoming feature films. So I hitched my trailer to their rides and spent the next year volunteering in the camera department on feature films across the state, learning under a number of fantastic cinematographers and camera assistants.

A simple trick I had picked up overhearing crew complain about new film attachments was to remind myself that I didn't know everything. Film attachments are usually young aspiring film students who are eager to gain hands-on experience in a short-term trainee role on set. Particularly as a film student, and having made a few short films myself, I was there to learn, not to impress. I decided from day one to be as teachable as possible: to ask questions, listen, and be as useful as I could. Unfortunately I watched other film students practically strut onto film sets with the confidence of their 'film education', only to be fired within the week for their arrogant 'know-all' attitude.

Chairman and CEO of Xero, Anne Mulcahy says: 'I am still learning. That is an important mark of a good leader… to know you don't know it all and never will.'

Over the following twelve months, I juggled working on feature films and university work. As I became more engaged with the former, I became less interested in the latter. But being someone who loved academia, I was torn by the idea of dropping out of university and not getting a degree. Though I knew many people who learnt on the job instead of through a formal education, and it had worked out great for them, after twelve years of being a very diligent student, I thought I would be leaving university with a degree in hand. But could the school of life perhaps be a better education for me?

My tipping point came in the form of a short film directed by one of the uni lecturers. I was volunteering on the production of the film as the second camera assistant (2nd AC). The role of a 2nd is predominantly to lug around camera equipment, manage data (it used to be film reels when I started, but the technological advancements were quickly transforming the industry to digital at the time) and, most famously, mark the slate. The slate, or clapper board, is a small whiteboard that you'd write the shot number on, with a pair of black-and-white marker sticks on top. The 2nd AC holds the slate in front of the camera at the start of each shot, calls out the shot details on cue and claps together the sticks to allow the editor to synchronise the footage with the audio during post-production. Having just come off a seven-week feature film working under one of the country's best first assistant cameras (1st AC), I had become very familiar with slating efficiently and so was more than happy to help out on this uni production.

As the sun rose and shone through the frosty grass on the first day of filming, we all prepared for the cameras to start rolling. The first assistant director (1st AD) hushed the crew as normal, and announced we were going for a take. 'Quiet on set, here we go ... and roll sound,' she declared.

'Sound speed,' the sound recordist responded, indicating that the audio was now recording. I held out the freshly marked-up slate in front of the camera lens and clearly stated, 'Scene four, shot one, take one.' I awaited the words, 'Mark it' from the camera operator who had hit the record button and was now ready. I clapped the two sticks together, ducked out of the way and the 1st AD announced, 'Action.' We were off.

But once 'Cut' was called and we finished the shot, the director halted the film set and, in front of all of the cast and crew, informed me that I was slating wrong. In the moment I was genuinely surprised, but being a teachable person, I quickly tried to hide my reaction and listened intently. He instructed me in the correct way to do it, according to the uni. His method was actually quite out of date and one that was used only within the bubble of our university. As a student of film, I was pretty horrified. What was the point of insisting upon a method that wasn't industry standard, especially as all of our goals were to graduate and work professionally in the film industry. I tucked away my pride, thanked him, and dutifully did as I was told for the remainder of the weekend. I immediately knew that I wasn't climbing the right ladder.

I quit university first thing the following Monday morning.

I had worked out that volunteering was the best way to break into this notoriously competitive and difficult industry. I would volunteer on as many films and TV commercials as I could to learn as much as possible, and hopefully secure another work opportunity out of each project.

My rationale was that if I could make myself available to work without needing to be paid, it would make it more appealing for producers to give me a shot and I could get what I needed—experience and connections. I did a quick calculation and figured that if I remained living at home with Mum and Dad and worked a certain number of hours each week at my part-time kitchen-hand job (the one I had started with Chris many years prior), I would have enough money to cover petrol for Dad's car that he'd lent me and I could drive myself to film sets. I mentally set aside two years to give this plan my best shot.

I had kept in touch with one particular line producer from that first short film with Tony. He was a very hard worker and was a lovely person, so would undoubtedly be going places. Since first meeting him, I would drop him an email every couple of weeks to politely check in and see if there were any projects I could help out on. I had learnt that I had to initiate these opportunities as they were unlikely to come to me. I wanted to stay top of mind.

Two months into my two-year plan, I was assisting a friend on a commercial shoot when the line producer called me with exciting news. 'I have a role on Scott's film,' he explained, 'but it's only for one week, not the whole shoot, if you want it?' I knew exactly what project he was talking about. The biggest film of the year in South Australia had just started three months of principal photography. Director Scott Hicks was filming an Australian/British drama called *The Boys Are Back* starring Clive Owen. Everyone I knew had tried to get a spot on the crew but nearly all of the roles had already been filled with more experienced Sydney and Melbourne crew.

I finished my current job and started the very next week. I would be assisting the video split operator who had flown in from interstate, but was struggling to keep up due to the size of the project. It was a big crew, filming in lots of locations and was moving fast. Even though it was just one week, my plan was to come in and make myself as useful as possible. If I could make a space just my size by being as proactive and helpful as possible, then maybe they'd notice when I was gone the following week and want me back.

When we worked on set, we all talked on radios with earpieces and had our own radio channel for each department. The pressure was high and my new boss's frustration would quickly surface and he'd regularly yell confusing instructions at me through our radios. He didn't take good care of his tools so things kept breaking down. And his short temper didn't help either. On numerous occasions, the entire film production would come to a stand-still as he tried to work out ongoing problems with his equipment. I kept my cool, pre-emptively assisting any way I could, but by the end of the week, he was unravelling. He hadn't worked on a project of this scale before and it was showing.

On the Friday night we packed up for the week and I said my farewells to my new colleagues. My contract hadn't been extended so I was finishing up. I was sad I wouldn't be able to continue on the project, but grateful for the experience. The cinematographer, Greig Fraser ACS ASC, was an absolute master and I had thoroughly enjoyed learning from him by watching how he interacted with the director, positioned the camera, worked with his camera team and shaped light in each space. I thanked the line producer for the opportunity and he kindly assured me we'd keep in touch in the coming months.

But I hadn't expected to hear from him so soon. Early the next morning, my phone rang and the sound of the line producer's voice was a very welcome surprise. 'They want you back,' he said quickly. 'The producers fired the video split operator last night and they're flying in a new operator and his assistant from Sydney. But the producers wanted to see if you'd like to stay on as the assistant instead?' By the end of that first week, the camera department had noticed the 'Henry-shaped space' I had made. At one point during a chaotic moment on set when the production was once again waiting for the video split operator, the 1st AC had switched his radio over to our channel to try and understand the cause of the hold up and had heard my boss flying off the handle at me. On the Friday night after work, the 1st AC had met with the producers and fought for me to stay. I was elated.

Tim, the new operator, was flown in that night and he spent the Sunday briefing me on how he liked to work and taught me how to use all of his equipment. Immediately, he was noticeably different to the previous operator—he was collected, organised, efficient and communicated clearly. No more blaming equipment breakdowns and yelling through radio earpieces. I signed a new contract for the remainder of the film and stepped back on set on Monday morning.

The production was a three-month whirlwind of an education. I was learning more about filmmaking each day than I had after eighteen months at university. The crew were the highest calibre I had ever met, using equipment I had never seen before. Entire houses were built as sets, camera cranes were mounted on the back of specialised trucks, sections of the city were shut down so we could film and I was fulfilling my university dreams to meet other filmmakers and learn how to make great films as a team.

By the end of the three months, I was exhausted and fulfilled. I had worked as hard as I could and learnt a huge amount. We spent the last week of production filming pickup shots on sound stages where sections of sets from the film had been recreated to capture important moments that were missed during production. On the final Friday afternoon, 'Cut' was called for the last time and we were done. I was simultaneously exhilarated and completely sapped. It was my biggest role yet and I felt like I had finally broken into the film industry. But from the next morning I would be unemployed again and back to regularly emailing producers.

As Tim and I packed up his equipment in the carpark and prepared for him to return to Sydney the following day, he pulled me aside and asked me seriously, 'Do you want to come and work for me in Sydney? I've been looking for an assistant for some time,' he continued, while I tried my best to hide my eagerness, 'and I haven't found one as good as you.' For the second time on this project, I was elated by the prospect of employment. Without a second thought, and probably delivered with way too much enthusiasm, I responded, 'Yes, of course!'

I had two weeks to pack up my life in Adelaide, say goodbye to everyone I loved and relocate to the east coast. I had given myself two years to break into the film industry and here I was, getting ready to move over to Sydney after just five months. By positioning myself to be able to volunteer and work as hard as I could, I had the opportunity to create a space just my size. One more step upwards on the ladder, and it was the right ladder!

TAKEAWAYS

Ensure you are climbing the right ladder. You don't want to get to the top only to realise that it was leaning up against the wrong building.

Remain teachable always. An important mark of a good leader is to know that you don't know it all and never will.

Maximise learning. Before demanding to be paid, set yourself up to be able to learn and absorb as much as you can, even if that means volunteering for a period to get your foot in the door.

Create a space just your size. By being a positive addition to those around you, you create a space just your size. So that if you leave, others will miss your contribution and presence and want you back.

CHAPTER SIX | **STARTUP**

How to Jump Without a Parachute

Operating in our purpose is extremely fulfilling. It just feels right. But it's not always easy or straightforward.

In January 2009, I arrived in a very hot and humid Sydney. Coming from the hot but dry summer weather of the Adelaide Hills, I wasn't prepared for the sweat-inducing humidity of the coast. By mid-morning each day, my clothes would be saturated with perspiration and so, begrudgingly, I spent the little money I had on upgrading my wardrobe with outdoor active clothing more intended for these tropical climates.

Sydney was an exciting place for a twenty-year-old. Four times larger than Adelaide, it had completely overwhelmed me on my trips as a kid. I was extremely fortunate to have relatives who lived thirty minutes out of the city and had kindly offered for me to come and stay with them. They had four kids; three were older than me and had moved out, so they had a couple of spare bedrooms.

Greater Sydney was too big to take in straight away. The famous Harbour Bridge and the Opera House, Chinatown, Cockatoo Island, Bondi Beach, the inner-west, Northern Beaches, the train systems, the ferries. It was a big place. But I had one of the best tour guides a newcomer could ask for. Working for Tim and his business partner Damon, I assisted them both on big-budget TV commercials. Compared to a three-month feature film, these one-to three-day shoots were lightning fast. And each shoot was with a different crew and at a different location. So every day we were filming in another fascinating part of Sydney that allowed me to get to know the area very well.

After a couple of months of having me assist on shoots, they began training me up to be the main operator, which meant they could send me out on jobs solo. Being a video split operator hadn't been a part of my plan but it allowed me to meet the best film technicians in Sydney and work on ads for well-known brands. I got to work on commercials for supermarkets, cars, fast food restaurants, cereal, soy milk and raisin toast. Fully enrolled now as a student in the school of life, my filmmaking knowledge and experience increased quickly. My teachers were some of the best directors, producers and cinematographers in the country. We were working with the best equipment and locations money could buy and a rotating panel of demanding clients on set every day were harsher than any lecturer marking assignments. It was a thrive or die environment and I was loving it!

My biggest challenge though was not on set. I was lonely. Big cities like Sydney are very difficult places to meet people. Unlike in smaller cities, everyone I met was busy and striving after their career aspirations. Even though I was working with different film crews every day, I was the youngest by a good ten years on nearly every job so I struggled to find friends my own age.

In August, an exciting work opportunity came in. A big feature film was gearing up for production and they wanted us to provide the video split services. For many years, various producers had approached author John Marsden to turn his beloved teenage survival novels, *The Tomorrow Series*, into a series of action-packed feature films. He had been unhappy with how they had planned to adapt his work until he received a scripted version of his first book, Tomorrow When the War Began, from Hollywood screenwriter Stuart Beattie. Beattie had come from writing Pirates of the Caribbean, Collateral and Australia. With John's blessing, the film had been given the green light and would be filming for four months in and around Sydney.

Tim and Damon felt I was ready to operate solo on a feature and, so two weeks later, I arrived at Fox Studios for our first day of filming. I had been assigned an assistant, Adam, by the production and, remembering my initial training with Tim back in Adelaide, I quickly brought him up to speed. The film was definitely the biggest I had ever worked on so I was equally terrified and excited.

For half of the four-month production schedule, we were filming three hours north of Sydney in the Hunter Valley. The area is known for its beautiful countryside so it was a perfect location for this rural-set film. There was only one problem with being away from Sydney so much ... I had just met a girl.

Rewind a couple of months and an emerging filmmaker called Genevieve had just created a film about a young man with Down syndrome at a bus stop. Having entered it into Australia's largest short film festival, Tropfest, the film had just won Best Film and Genevieve was getting a lot of attention. One opportunity that came her way was from a large music publishing company to create a video for a new band. The budget wasn't particularly large so, instead of creating a concept that would require a whole film crew to produce, she cleverly resolved to create an animation that could be done with only a small number of people. Maybe even just one.

Through mutual friends, she had heard that I had been animating projects by myself and got a hold of my number. She rang me one afternoon while I was working back at Tim and Damon's office. To be honest, I thought she was a little deluded. It was clear she hadn't created an animation before, and she had unrealistic visions for this project. Regardless, I agreed to meet up and chat about the project.

We met on a Sunday afternoon. For late winter, it was a typically warm Sydney day, something I was still acclimatising to. Genevieve had chosen a cafe that was on her way home from her church in the city. As I walked inside there was only one woman sitting at a table, so I presumed it was her. Knowing very little about her, I was expecting to meet with a much older woman. Instead, I was faced with a beautiful twenty-year-old girl who looked up and beamed as I walked in. Before I even sat down, I was smitten.

I channelled every bit of energy I had to stay professional and cool. We spoke in depth about her project, the sorts of films she liked to make, movies and music we liked, faith and spirituality, moving to Sydney for work and making films that matter. Before we had even finished our meeting, I knew I had just met the woman I wanted to marry.

As we readied to leave, I took my opportunity to see if we could spend more time together in the not-so-distant future. After all, I barely knew anyone my own age in this city, let alone another filmmaker with similar values. 'I don't mean to be too forward,' I began, in probably not my best linguistic manoeuvre, 'but I was wondering if we could hang out?' To this day, Genevieve stands by the fact that I was asking her out. A very hasty move for a first business meeting, but in my defence, even though I was already besotted with her, I was genuinely just looking for some friends my own age to spend time with.

In a kind attempt to deflect my proposition without damaging my ego, she quickly responded, 'Why don't you come to church with me one weekend? You can come and meet some of my friends.' I didn't need to be asked twice.

Over the next couple of weeks I tried to play it cool, desperately attempting to hide my level of attraction to Genevieve. I was so happy to be able to hang out with her and her friends, spending time with people my own age who similarly had all moved to Sydney for work opportunities.

I soon discovered that she wasn't interested in dating. I had learnt this the hard way after a few weeks when I had finally plucked up the courage to ask her out to dinner and she was clear that she wasn't looking for a romantic relationship. To add salt to the wound, our music video project fell through. The client had pulled the budget and disappeared, never to be heard from again. But I wasn't going to let this put an end to our relationship.

We had both recognised the creative spark between us and wanted to see what it could turn into. Our skills complemented each other perfectly—she wrote and directed, and I shot and edited. We set about filming a documentary about a blind busker Genevieve had met in the commuter tunnels underneath Sydney Central train station. We used every spare moment we had to work on the film. Then the feature film in the Hunter Valley landed.

So for two months while I was filming on location for the feature, I would drive the three hours back to Sydney each Friday night as soon as we wrapped. When the film moved into two weeks of night shoots, where we'd finish at 6 am each Saturday morning, this made for a less than delightful drive back home.

As we got towards the end of production on the feature film, life was starting to look really good. Genevieve had been working late nights at her production role with a TV network so, after work each night, I had left packages filled with home-cooked meals on her doorstep. Then on my third attempt asking her out, Genevieve finally agreed to a date with me. The home cooking must have been the tipping point.

During the same period, Genevieve had also just received a call from a different TV network. They were going to be producing a TV show loosely based on *The Amazing Race* where pairs of filmmakers would travel around the world to competitively make short films and they had shortlisted her to be a part of the show.

At first she pushed away the offer. She already had a stable production job and didn't want to risk upsetting the apple cart. But they continued to persist, eventually telling Genevieve they had fast-tracked her past the shortlist stage and had selected her as one of the final candidates. The gig was hers for the taking— all she had to do was quit her current job. Genevieve began to entertain the idea of making short films around the world and she called me to ask if I would be interested in going with her. An easy answer! The timing would work well for me as it would start production straight after we wrapped on *Tomorrow When the War Began*.

So she decided to jump in and accept the role. The TV execs were thrilled and instructed her to submit her resignation straight away and fly down to Melbourne two days later to talk through the finer details. She handed in her notice that day and we began to get excited about our forthcoming global adventures. The next step in our filmmaking journeys was looking very promising, until the very next morning the inevitable happened.

The TV execs called her back but with bad news. The whole show had been cancelled. The network had pulled the funding and everything had been shut down overnight. We were dumbfounded. This had been such a sure thing and we'd been told everything was locked in and ready to go. We had seen the pathway laid out in front of us. What was worse, Genevieve couldn't reverse her resignation and even though they wanted to, there was nothing her bosses could do about it either. She was out on the street without any work.

Once we'd taken the time to process the shock of being left high and dry, Genevieve and I began to talk about what could be next and what sort of production roles we should apply for. Living in Sydney, one of the most expensive cities in the world, was no walk in the park so we needed jobs to be able to cover our rent. But there was a thought niggling at the back of my mind—we both had dreams of creating content that we were passionate about. Could there be a way that we could get paid to make our own projects? We wanted to create films and stories that could positively impact the world, not just sell home insurance and raisin toast.

'Why don't we take a leap of faith and start a production company ourselves?' I asked one evening. We didn't know the first thing about running a business but we knew that, together, we were a great team and even better storytellers.

I was about to learn an important lesson. To be an entrepreneur and start your own business is like jumping out of an aeroplane with only the individual parts of a parachute in your hands: you make the leap and have to figure out how to assemble it before you hit the ground. In the Bible, it says that if you wait for the perfect conditions, you will never get anything done*. These certainly were not perfect conditions, but we were ready to jump.

I finished up the feature film, gratefully thanked Tim and Damon for seeing potential in me and handed in my resignation.

---

* Like a yokel reviewing Shakespeare, please excuse my poor simplified version. Look up Ecclesiastes for a much wiser, better written pocketful of wisdom.

Genevieve and I stood on the threshold of the aeroplane's open door, held each other's hand and jumped.

A pair of wide-eyed and optimistic twenty-year-olds, we started our production company on a very hot Sydney summer's morning. And when I say 'started', from the outside there would not be much evidence of a functioning company for some time. But we started, and our little production company called Taste Films (which would later change to Taste Creative) was born.

It was the first Monday of 2010. While others were welcoming in the new year with friends at the park or surfing down at the beach, we began setting up an office in the run-down spare room off the side of Genevieve's bedroom in Petersham, a quiet inner-west suburb ten minutes out of Sydney CBD. Not quite big enough to be a two-person office, the room was more of an oversized walk-in wardrobe. But for us, it was ours. And it was perfect.

I had $7,000 of savings from the past year that we used as seed money and we needed this to last us for as long as possible. We purchased two cheap desks from Ikea, repurposed my grandma's old wardrobe as a film equipment cupboard and screwed up two wooden planks to the wall for shelving. Office: check.

Now what?

One afternoon, as Genevieve was walking back to her house, she spotted a poster in the window of a government services building. It read, 'Do you want to get paid to work in your business? Study with us today.' The Australian Government was offering a training program called The New Enterprise Incentive Scheme (NEIS) to help new small businesses start and stay afloat*. Once you completed their course in small business management they would pay you a basic salary for a year to work in your business. The fact was, and currently is, that the majority of small businesses will fail and close down in their first two years. Most new small business owners need to have a part-time job alongside their startup just so they can cover their basic bills like food and rent, which means that they can only dedicate a few hours a week to actually work in their own business. So joining NEIS was a no-brainer.

---

* NEIS is still operating today and is a really great incentive for people wanting to start a business—I promise I haven't even been paid to say that. It's genuinely an amazing government initiative in Australia.

Genevieve and I signed up straight away. The course provided us with the basics of how to start a business and what we needed to think about for growth in the future. Together, we learnt and implemented the imperative distinction between working in our business and working on our business. We even turned every Wednesday into a WOB day (working on the business) to focus on establishing our company processes and values. We devoured chapters of Michael E. Gerber's business handbook, *The E Myth Revisited*, and set about planning not just short-term survival, but what sort of business we wanted it to grow into in the years to come.

Even with no clients or projects yet, Genevieve and I would work diligently in and on our business every day, Monday to Friday. Come 5.30 pm, we would leave our small office, shut the door and get on with the night. Many times we were tempted to keep working into the evening and just grab a bite to eat on the go rather than 'leave the office', but this separation of home and work was really helpful. We were still newly dating and working from Genevieve's house, so it became really important to define the boundaries between work and personal life, and then try our hardest to stick to them.

From the few interviews I'd heard with successful entrepreneurs, many had talked about the importance of cultivating not just a healthy mind but also a healthy body so Genevieve and I figured we'd better get started ourselves. Though likely not frequently enough to make a big health impact, Genevieve and I would sporadically go for an early morning run around our neighbourhood to get the heart rate up. On our weaving path through Sydney's inner-west, we would jog past the office of a small video production company. Heralded by a handsome metal sign hanging out the front of the building, we would stare longingly through the windows at what we considered to be 'a real business'. They had six work desks (which at the time felt like an unfathomably high number of staff), plants in hanging baskets, shiny new Apple computers and graphics tablets and a sea of coloured sticky notes stuck to the wall from what looked like a high-octane creative brainstorm. From all that we could tell, they had it all.

We'd go back to the two Ikea desks in our cramped home office and it was difficult not to compare ourselves. It became so easy to look at how well other businesses were doing, or at least how they appeared on the outside, and compare with our own measly achievements. To be able to stay on track, we had to quickly learn how to swim in our own lane and stop comparing ourselves with what other people were doing. So we focussed on what was in front of us and became intentional about celebrating our own wins, no matter how small and no matter what our circumstances were telling us.

One very ordinary afternoon, a large pharmaceutical company called us needing some help to create a video. They had seen Genevieve's film festival win and were keen to get our assistance as filmmakers. So after we had conducted our first real client meeting, we made sure to acknowledge this big achievement for our little company and took the time to celebrate. Seeing as we didn't have much money, we took ourselves down the road to the cafe at the other end of the block and bought a homemade pie to share. Compared to our usual lunch of peanut butter on toast or a tin of tuna and salad, this shared pie was sensational.

On future occasions, we would pool together our loose change and share a fresh coconut from the same cafe. The owner, a Thai chef, would order in these whole coconuts, split the top off in front of you and hand us a straw and a spoon to devour it. Having so little at the time, these coconuts were unbelievable!

Without realising it, we had stumbled upon a crucial value to be able to be happy. As the both of us were perfectionists in our work, we had discovered that we didn't need to wait until every problem was solved to be able to be happy—instead we would find any reason to celebrate. This helped ensure that we could find joy in every working day, even on the really tough days, which of course there were plenty of.

But a really great day came our way after about ten months. At a 'Women in Business' event, Genevieve had coincidentally sat next to a woman who she had briefly met before. Naturally they got talking and Genevieve shared the vision for our business and talked about what we had been working on. It turned out that this woman, Wendy Simpson—a serial entrepreneur responsible for the successful growth of a number of large global companies—was interested in what we were doing and wanted to come around to our office to meet us both.

The morning of our meeting, we scrambled to tidy the house and make it feel as professional and 'officey' as possible. Unfortunately to reach our office, you had to walk through Genevieve's bedroom so from the get-go it wasn't the most professional first impression. But Wendy didn't mind in the slightest. She loved startup businesses and was much more interested in the vision and the people behind them.

Both Genevieve and I were hungry to learn from people who had already walked paths similar to the one we were on, so we welcomed Wendy's interest in our business. Australian author and evangelist Phil Pringle would often say, 'If you want to get wet, stand under a waterfall. Find people that you want to learn from, and spend as much time as you can around them.'

As we sat crammed into our little office with cups of tea perched on our desks, Wendy listened intently to our business plans, looked at our films and some of the commercial videos we had been producing and asked lots of questions about our purpose and personal drivers. We told her of our passion to tell stories that could impact people from all over the world. She took one look around the room and said, 'You need a bigger office for that vision.' With a final sip from her teacup, she narrowed in on us both: 'Why don't you come and work out of my office for a little bit and I can give you some pointers?'

We had found our first waterfall.

Having recently sold the manufacturing business she had run for many years with her husband, Wendy and he had always been passionate about investing their resources into young people. An incredible couple, Wendy and Geoff had previously fostered thirteen at-risk teenagers over many years and now they had turned their passion for sharing their wisdom to empowering young entrepreneurs.

For many years, I have wondered why Wendy and Geoff chose to invest their time, knowledge and guidance in us. I have never had a concrete answer from them, but I am grateful that Genevieve attended that 'Women in Business' breakfast all those years ago. People like Wendy and Geoff became a lifeline for us. Even though they weren't from the same industry, or even a similar field, they had great wisdom regarding how to run a business, working with suppliers, developing staff, cash flow management and pitching for work.

One of the first gems that Wendy insisted we understand was a thing called 'an entrepreneurial mindset'. When we are an employee, paid to work in someone else's organisation, we don't need to carry the weight of their business on our shoulders.

At the end of the work day we stand up, walk away and get on with our own lives. Our bosses would be lucky if we spared a second thought about the functioning of their business before we return to work the next day. But as an entrepreneur, we don't switch off at 5.30 pm. If problems aren't solved or there are issues that need attention, it is the business owner's responsibility to do something about it.

This mentality calls for a shift to an 'always on' mindset. This isn't an excuse to be a workaholic; rather it is the responsibility we take on when birthing a company of our own. While the hardworking attitude had come naturally to Genevieve and I, it was a revelation to learn that other people found this strange. At times we had even felt ostracised from those around us. We missed many family events, weren't able to stay long at friends' parties and just couldn't commit to giving the same amount of time that we used to give to old and new relationships. Like a parent of a newborn child, we had to focus on doing what we had to do to ensure our business could grow.

Years later, we had a lemon tree in our backyard that became very special to us. I had bought the tree as a sapling so it already had a healthy growth of small branches and leaves, but no fruit yet. I cared for it dearly, planting it in rich fertilisers, watering it regularly and feeding it fresh worm tea from my backyard worm farm, it took pride of place in the sunniest spot in the centre of our inner-city courtyard. I loved to watch its development and would check on it almost daily to see how it was progressing. For months and months I barely saw any growth and I gradually stopped checking on it daily*. But one day, about two years later while sitting in the courtyard, I suddenly realised how much the tree had grown and how much bigger it was compared to when I had bought it.

That spring, dozens of little white flowers began appearing on all the branches, and by winter, I had a crop of gorgeous big lemons. If the tree had started flowering too early without the tree growing enough both above and beneath the soil, the tree would have failed. It would have only been able to produce small, inedible fruit or, if it had grown large fruit, the small branches would have snapped under the weight. And then if the roots hadn't gone down far enough, the tree itself would have blown over in the first storm that passed overhead.

---

*   This is probably for the best. If lemon trees could talk, I'm sure this one would have said I was suffocating it. I was the classic lemon tree helicopter parent.

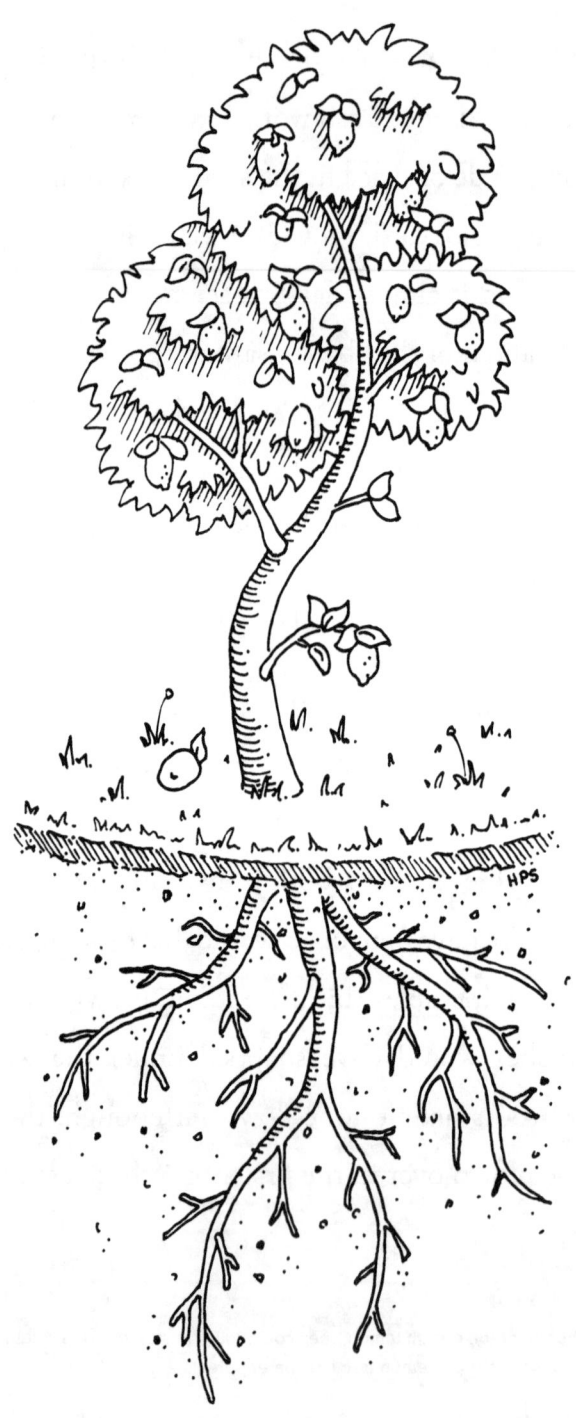

Imperative to the success of our lemon tree was not just what we could see above the surface but, just as critical, was what was growing under the soil.

In our business we knew we had to do the same thing. We gave ourselves the first twelve months to focus on nothing more than putting down our roots. We weren't concerned about how people might perceive our work yet or the criticism that we spent too much time working on our business. We had our attention fixed on what they couldn't see—the foundations. We were teaching ourselves how to develop a business plan, how to work with clients, how we would manage staff, build healthy work cultures and set up the systems to pay people.

But the biggest thing I focussed on was my own character. When asked why many great leaders don't make the distance, American author Ed Stetzer shared that the problem lies in character, or a lack of its development. He recounts: 'There's a body count of young [leaders] whose ability rose them to prominence before their character was ready for it.'

I wanted to make sure that our characters were grounded and strong enough so that when opportunities arose or, on the flip side, when the storms came (when, not if), we wouldn't blow over in the wind.

I chose to see every major challenge that came our way as an opportunity to strengthen our foundations. Very often this was not an easy or automatic decision, but we were intentional in retraining our brains to practise this way of thinking. Big issues that arose weren't roadblocks, but became learning opportunities. Yes, they were very difficult, but I would think, I'd much rather learn this lesson on a project this size than on a project with a couple more zeros at the end of the budget!

This approach has served us exceptionally well. We have journeyed through countless storms, from personal and professional relationship breakdowns and extremely difficult clients, to managing under-performing staff out of the business, and navigating detrimental cash flow issues. We certainly didn't do everything perfectly but we were able to journey through and survive the storms. Having taken the time to intentionally build solid foundations has ensured that we have stayed rooted and not toppled over. Which is fortunate because as we began the journey to turn our dreams into reality, it was apparent that our path would not always be clear.

TAKEAWAYS

If you wait for the perfect conditions, you will never start. Being an entrepreneur is like jumping out of a plane with only the pieces of a parachute, and you have to learn how to assemble it on the way down.

Working on the business is just as important as working in the business. Taking the time to establish strong and deep foundations will help to see you and your business through the challenging times when they arise.

Separate work and home. Particularly for start-up businesses or working from home, it is imperative to define the boundaries not just for you, but for the betterment of the people you live with.

Take the time to celebrate. Even if you don't have the means, just acknowledging the wins, no matter how small, is important to mark momentum and progress. Find any reason to celebrate.

If you want to get wet, stand under a waterfall. Find the people that you want to learn from and spend as much time as you can around them.

CHAPTER SEVEN | BENEFITING OTHERS

The Earth Didn't Tremble, But the World Changed

There are certain introductions to people that you can pinpoint as pivotal moments. When Genevieve met Gerard, each of our futures would be drastically changed for the better. From their single meeting alone, I would then spend fifteen years following their encounter, discovering that a central part of my purpose was not for my benefit, but for many others.

Just a few months before Genevieve and I had met, she had met another young man. She was in her final year of her university film degree* and she had secured a role directing a documentary

---

* Genevieve's university experience was way better than mine, so she was much more enthusiastic to stick it out to completion. So much so that she went on to do her postgraduate degree and a Masters in Film Direction. You can probably tell—I'm only a tad jealous.

for Down syndrome Australia (DSA). The film was showcasing the stories of a number of people with Down syndrome and their support networks. She was a couple of months into filming when DSA rang her to say there was another participant they thought would be good for the doco and would she go and meet with him?

Obligingly, Genevieve set out to the western suburbs of Sydney. She found the correct house and, when she knocked on the front door, a young man with Down syndrome named Gerard O'Dwyer appeared. Instead of one of the more usual greetings we've become accustomed to expect, Gerard erupted into a full Shakespeare soliloquy on his doorstep. Deploying character voices and dramatic arm gestures, he recited the entire balcony scene from *Romeo and Juliet* off by heart.

Gerard was a passionate amateur actor with an incredible memory for long scenes of dialogue from movies and television, including *The Lion King*, *Harry Potter*, and his favourite, *The Bold and the Beautiful*. But because he had a disability, no one had given him an opportunity to perform. They may have thought that they were being kind, but everyone had told him he'd never make it as an actor and it was best to give up on his dream of performing to avoid disappointment. But, luckily, his new friend Genevieve was not like everyone else.

Back at uni, Genevieve had been due to create her final short film for the end-of-year showcase. She already had a concept in mind, but as soon as she'd met Gerard, she knew she wanted to give him an opportunity to star in her film. She threw away her script and wrote a new idea that would feature Gerard in the lead role. Genevieve also felt passionately that if she was going to tell a story about the disability community, then they should be represented not just in front of the camera, but also behind the camera so as to influence how the film got made. So she put up an ad that read, 'If you have a disability and want to learn about filmmaking, let me know!' Five young people with disability applied and she ran a very basic introduction to filmmaking course in her friend's living room.

Leading up to filming Genevieve heard plenty of cynicism and criticism. She was told the film would be a failure; working with people with a disability would slow down production; it would cost more money; the film itself would be no good. Genevieve knew what the right thing to do was, so turned a deaf ear to the doubters and pushed on. On a set comprising a bus stop overlooking a river, each of the filmmaking students was mentored by a crew member and the film was shot successfully on schedule and came in under budget.

When Genevieve entered the finished film into Australia's largest short film festival, not only did it win Best Film overall, but Gerard won Best Male Actor in front of 250,000 people. Gerard had found his platform, Genevieve disproved the critics and inclusive filmmaking was born.

By this point, I still hadn't met Genevieve. It wasn't until early the next morning that I got to hear her voice for the very first time. She was interviewed on the radio about her big win and I listened to her jubilant voice as I drove past the Fish Markets in Sydney on my way to a TV commercial shoot. I had no idea that our paths were about to cross and that my future would dramatically change.

Genevieve had captured the life-changing experience from that first inclusive film set. Fast-forward twelve months and she had turned it into a film school for marginalised people. A cohort of twelve young people living with disability became the first class of Bus Stop Films and in the lead-up to the end of their first year, they were ready to produce their first professional film as a class. Students would be able to put all of their theoretical knowledge into practice.

Genevieve co-wrote a ten-minute script with all of the students and then needed some help to bring the film to life. A priority for us was to ensure the film did not look like a low-quality community project. It needed to look and feel as professional and high quality as any other film in a top-tier film festival. So I reached out to all of my newly found contacts from the TV commercials I had been working on. Each was at the top of their field and it was a big ask—not just to come and crew the film, but we were asking them to come into class to teach a three-hour workshop about their craft. To my amazement, people were delighted. No one had ever asked them to share their wisdom and knowledge like this before. So we held mini masterclasses on sound recording, lighting, camera, wardrobe and makeup in the lead-up to our film.

The day of filming itself was an absolute success. We were, of course, a bit nervous about whether or not it would work, but by the time we rolled the camera for the first shot in a high-rise lobby in the middle of Sydney, each student had been paired up with their mentor and everyone was busy at work.

In the course of just one day, the traditional film hierarchy was shattered. As the director sitting at the top of the pyramid, everyone saw how Genevieve worked with those under her and they all followed suit. At one point, she offered to make a cup of tea for the production assistant and I saw the reactions of amazement from our long-time professionals on set. This was not at all how things work on a traditional film set, but we were redefining how _our_ film sets would work. The spirit of inclusion was infectious and everyone had caught the bug.

The film itself, *The Interviewer*, went on to win awards at film festivals around the world and clock up over forty million views on YouTube. Over ten years later, we are still working with many of the same crew from this film, who all delight in working on our inclusive productions. I knew the experience would be a great opportunity for the students, but I underestimated the impact it would have on the crew. A large number of them have since gone on to create ongoing roles and opportunities for people with a disability to work on their own commercial projects as well. Through just one project, I could clearly see that our purpose really does thrive when it is benefiting others.

For the first seven years of Taste Creative, we incubated Bus Stop Films to ensure it had the best possible opportunity to survive. We believed in the notion of inclusive filmmaking but knew it would take time for it to be strong enough to stand on its own. Taste received just as much from Bus Stop as it did in return. Having the two companies working side by side infused our values and culture, and the spirit of inclusion permeated everything we did. Teaching and collaborating with students with a disability became an everyday occurrence for our staff and our pool of freelancers looked forward to mentoring students on our projects.

We applied the same principles of inclusion to every project we did. From disability service providers and not-for-profits, to supermarkets, cruise lines and telecom providers, it didn't matter the industry, inclusion always made sense. When we were asked to create a brand film for a customer-owned bank, we intuitively presented a campaign that featured the customers and their stories using our inclusive process to involve them in every stage of the filmmaking journey and the campaign was a hit.

Inclusion just became second nature for all of our staff. From their hands-on experience, our team would think about accessibility of our films from the very beginning—did everyone, regardless of their ability level, have the opportunity to enjoy our work?

Our first opportunity to take our inclusive filmmaking model beyond our Australian shores came off of the back of *The Interviewer*. The film's universal message had been received so well at film festivals around the world—amongst the many awards that it had won, it was honoured as Best Film at the Short Shorts Film Festival in Japan. The festival is one of the largest short film festivals in Asia and is accredited by the Academy Awards®. Each year the festival runs an invite-only competition for previous winners of the Best Film category. Filmmaking teams are invited to pitch a short film to be shot in Tokyo to help promote the city to the world. After winning the category with *The Interviewer*, we had been invited to submit each year since but had just been too busy to get involved.

After a couple of years of no submissions from us, the Program Director reached out directly to try and persuade us to submit an idea for that year's competition. Again we looked at our full diaries and had to apologetically decline. But he persisted and persisted and so, one evening, Genevieve and I decided to sit up late and put together a proposal based around a story starring our good friend Gerard. We posed a simple idea: what if a young man with Down syndrome has been taken to Tokyo on his older brother's business trip and he escapes to sneak off and explore the city on his own.

Up until this point, we were aware that people with disability had close to zero visibility throughout the Japanese film industry. In many parts of Asia, it would be very unlikely to see a person with disability in a TV commercial or a film, let alone working behind the scenes on a film set. But with nothing to lose, we presented our concept and explained that if we were to be successful, we would partner with a disability organisation in Tokyo and teach aspiring local filmmakers with disability how to work on a professional film. Nothing like this had ever been done before in Japan so we knew it was a bold move.

Three weeks later the festival's Program Director called us with the exciting news that our project had been selected. With little more than the film's premise, Genevieve and I were flown to Tokyo a few weeks later to meet with the team and flesh out the story. The film was to be funded by the Tokyo Metropolitan Government, and their brief was to showcase parts of Tokyo that people were unlikely to have seen before. So with the Program Director as our guide, we spent a week exploring many of the hidden gems of the sprawling city.

We gawked at ancient temples surrounded by gardens so dense that you'd forget you were in the middle of one of the world's busiest cities. We squeezed into tiny standing sushi bars with a sushi master whose hands were smoothed from sixty years of shaping sushi rice. We climbed ladders up into the crammed sake bars of the Golden Gai, rode the old ferries to the tea houses in the Hamarikyu Gardens and we shared traditional soba noodles presented on wooden trays as big as the table. In no time at all, we had a plethora of amazing locations in which to set our story.

Four months later we returned to Tokyo with Gerard, two of our regular film collaborators and Australian actor

Patrick Brammall to play Gerard's older brother. The rest of our cast and crew would be made up of locals from throughout Japan. Not speaking any Japanese, we quickly equipped ourselves with a handful of useful phrases that would guide us through production.

Our first task was to host our inclusive filmmaking workshops for the aspiring local filmmakers. We partnered with the Japan Down syndrome Society and, just as Genevieve had done in her friend's lounge room all those years prior, we hosted a filmmaking workshop with six ambitious filmmakers who had Down syndrome. This time Gerard was now one of the teachers and he revelled in his role. He masterfully shared his knowledge of character development and mise en scène and inspired the class with his passion and charisma.

Three days later we began capturing the film all across the city, featuring the famously busy Shibuya crossing*, rickshaw rides in Asakusa, high-rise towers with views to Mt Fuji and a hidden ramen restaurant tucked away in a back alley that only

---

* Fun fact: because our project was commissioned by the Tokyo Metropolitan Government, I was later told that we were the first ever film production to be granted an official permit to be able to shoot at the crossing and not get chased away by the local police.

the locals knew about. We showcased traditional *okonomiyaki* with local actress Shioli Kutsuna and were honoured to film with the late martial arts legend Shinichi Chiba who taught Gerard's character the art of sumi-e (Japanese ink painting). All the while, our group of film students from the Japan Down Syndrome Society worked on set with us as fully-fledged crew members.

It was the first time anything like this had ever been done in Japan. In the moment we didn't feel the earth tremble as a world first was happening because we were just using the skills and tools that we had at our fingertips. But because it was birthed from purpose, it all just came naturally.

TAKEAWAYS

Follow your gut. Just because someone doesn't think it will work, does not mean it cannot work.

Define your purpose. Remember what it is and apply it.

PART THREE

Leading with Purpose

CHAPTER EIGHT | LEADING

Leadership Came Naturally, But to Do It Well Was Another Thing Altogether

Back in our little startup office with barely enough room for just the two of us, I would dream of the days when other people would be part of our team. I couldn't connect the dots from where we were at the time to how we'd be able to afford a staff member or even where they'd sit. But I had a feeling that only once we could hire our first employee would it then start to feel like a real company.

At this stage, we had no means to be able to pay Genevieve and I a salary each week. We were pouring in all the time and effort that we could give to our business to ensure it had the best opportunity to survive. I vividly remember the terror when it dawned on me that to actually 'employ' another person, we'd have to pay them a salary. Every week. As in rain, hail or shine. Every week we would have to pay them. Regardless of whether we won a job that week or not, regardless of whether a client paid us on time or not, we'd need to pay them their salary. But what if we couldn't afford it for one week? A tough cashflow week, a late payment from a client, an emergency expense? The thought of letting someone down absolutely terrified me.

And then where would they sit? They certainly weren't going to be able to fit in our oversized wardrobe office. We'd need to rent a bigger space. But then what if we didn't have enough money to cover our rent each month? I felt as though I could see where we wanted to get to, but the leap from where we currently were seemed insurmountable.

Fortunately for us, by this point Wendy had seen something special in Genevieve and I and she wanted to see us get off the ground. After twelve months of working in the wardrobe office, we were offered a big break.

As one of the board members of an industrial development company in Sydney, Wendy had decided to lease a large office space next door to one of their latest construction sites so that she could be nearby to oversee the project. The space was far too big for the two desks of her and her assistant, so she offered the back section of the office to us.

And to solve the cash flow issues, we agreed to a pro rata deal of creative services in lieu of paying rent. Back in the early 2000s Google used to have a free architectural design program that would allow architectural enthusiasts like me to create basic 3D renders of buildings, complete with furniture and forlorn-looking human figures to provide scale. One afternoon, Wendy had seen me designing a layout for our new office and asked if I could build out 3D renders from the floor plans of the warehouse development she was managing. I'd never done anything to that scale, but my motto was to 'Say yes and figure it out later', so these 3D renders became payment for our rent.

Her office was a large room with a row of bookshelves along the back wall. Wendy told us that if we pulled all the shelves forward, we could create a semi-private office space roughly three by six metres for ourselves behind them. Although it was uncannily similar to Harry Potter's room tucked in under the stairs, it was a real office. And it was our own. We busied ourselves moving in our desks, wheeling in swivel chairs, setting up our computers and carrying in an old kitchen table we had found online for free. We added a pin-up board with inspirational images, an A3 printout of our new company logo blue-tacked to the wall and a coloured novelty lamp in the corner because nothing says 'creative office' like a whacky lamp, right? Now we were in business.

All we had to do now was wait for the phone to ring.

But of course it didn't just 'ring'. Literally because we didn't have an office phone, but even if we had, it wouldn't have rung. Unfortunately, the act of blue-tacking a printout of our logo up on the wall hadn't had the effect of a global media release announcing that we were ready for business. We had to get out and pound the pavement.

Unfortunately in my measly eighteen months at film school, there had been no lectures on how to actually make a living from filmmaking. And from what I could see of the entire course—had I stuck it out—the business side of film was rarely taught. So we had to work out how to use the skills we had in storytelling to help companies to achieve their goals.

Using the small community network that we had in Sydney, we asked the people we knew for introductions to people who worked in marketing, human resources or anyone in a company that might benefit from our services. Without an impressive creative portfolio, we had to invest time into getting to know people's businesses to be able to understand their challenges and come up with ways that film production could address them.

From one project to the next, the interest in our work slowly began to grow—a video to promote a film festival, an animation explaining the social media guidelines for a pharmaceutical company, a band that needed a music video shot on a shoestring budget. We even blacked-out the corner of our office to create a makeshift stop-motion studio to animate a promotional video for an international aid charity. We worked long days and many weekends, but were loving that people were paying us to do what we loved.

We soon hit a point that clients were asking us to do more than we could handle ourselves. People enjoyed working with us and so had asked for help with other creative services: could we help create their brochure, design a new logo, create a flyer and design their new stationery?* We had started as a film production company but were eager to please and it seemed ludicrous to turn down work. So of course we said 'yes' and would figure it out later.

And of course 'later' soon arrived. We had held out for as long as we could, but knew that we now needed to grow our team to keep up with the demand. We had met a promising designer who would be an ideal resource to help with all these design requests. We scrambled to put together an employee contract and company guidelines and then excitedly offered her a job, becoming our very first employee. But there was only one problem—there was nowhere for her to sit. And to add to our space problems, clients had started asking to come to meet us at our offices for meetings.

It was time for a bigger space. Again.

We liked the area we were in as it was halfway between the city and the airport and we'd figured that for any interstate

---

* This is back in the days when printed stationery was tantamount to being a real and trustworthy business! In the back of a drawer somewhere I still have boxes of old business cards that we printed years and years ago and barely ever used.

clients, our office would be an easy location to drop into on their way in or out of Sydney. So, hunting around in the area, we found a beautiful new studio just around the corner: exposed brick walls, high ceilings, wooden floorboards, big windows and, unlike our current dark office behind the bookshelves, it was bathed in natural light. The studio was situated in a creative complex amongst fashion designers, architects, a coffee company and photography studio. From the tiny office off Genevieve's bedroom to a ginormous commercial studio, this was a big jump forward.

We set about turning the space into the studio of our dreams with big wooden desks, a giant illustration of our own design as a feature wall, a boardroom for client meetings, a film edit suite and a lounge room to host clients for creative presentations. We found an old piano that someone was selling online for a dollar* and we forklifted it up into our new office and turned it into a window display with our logo emblazoned on the front for all to see. Now we felt like a real company.

---

* Full disclosure: it cost us an additional $150 to get a removalist to transport it, and then our landlord who owned a forklift had to hoist it up over the balcony to our second-floor office because it couldn't fit in the elevator and there was no way we were carrying a piano up the stairs!

Our first employee officially started, freelancers were working from the office with us and clients were coming and going with new projects and things they needed our help with. The new office was abuzz with activity.

What I didn't realise at the time was that this rapid company growth was fuelling an internal battle. I was struggling with my own insecurities and fought a particularly fierce fight with imposter syndrome, which our impressive new office only made more difficult. Every day I was anxious that someone would walk in and expose me as an unqualified and less than worthy leader. I had no training in business management, I had dropped out of university early, I hadn't worked a day in my life in a real production company, and now here I was running one.

So until that person came to expose me, I distracted myself by focusing on the people and projects in front of me. I was confident that we had the skills to create the things we were promising our clients and we would figure out each problem as it arose.

To help combat my insecurities, I was very fortunate to have started working with an exceptional business coach called Brian.

Introduced to me through Wendy, Brian is a big man with a keenly felt Irish heritage and immensely strong compassion for people. Preferring a bear hug to a handshake, Brian specialised in helping business leaders find the clarity they needed in any situation. Whenever he would call to touch base, I wouldn't need to rely on caller ID to know who was on the end of the line. 'Henry, it's Brian' would come his thick Irish accent, introducing himself on the phone every time without fail. I have now known Brian for over ten years and still today he announces himself on every call.

One of the many things Brian imparted to me was a personal mantra which I had to remind myself daily*: 'I will make the best decision with the information that I have at the time.' Meaning I need to make a decision, but I may only have limited information right now. So I need to make the best call that I can with what I currently know. If I get more information in the future, I can adjust accordingly. This gem of wisdom released me from the feeling that I had to know everything and it deflated the pressure that I had to make the right decision at

---

* To do Brian justice, make sure you're reading this part with a heavy Irish accent in your head. Think Colin Farrell, Liam Neeson or Brendan Gleeson and you're on the right track.

every turn. I was learning how to back myself; I could step out knowing that I would be able to figure it out. And if we get new information after a decision, then we could adjust the course as needed.

At the same time, Genevieve and I were continuing to learn how to produce content together, not just as business partners but also as husband and wife after we had married in 2011. Whenever we would tell people that we worked in business with our spouse, we would get responses on a spectrum from caution and mild surprise to bewilderment and horror. Not many were overly encouraging of the idea. But from the early years, we had set out a rule that served us well—our marriage was always to come before the business. If at any point something threatened this, we were both committed to walking away from the business and leaving it all behind.

I'd love to say that we were perfect at this, but we weren't. We were both so passionate about our company, creating fantastic content and achieving great results that the peace in our marriage was threatened many times. But at the end of a heated argument, we would remember our rule and put it down on the table as the trump card and we'd resolve to find a workaround to ensure we could keep our marriage intact, and then our business.

To be able to keep harmony in both our marriage and business, we applied a key rule to working professionally together: there can only be one leader at a time. This may sound obvious, but we had to figure this out for ourselves. Who the leader is will change from project to project, but we learnt that we needed to identify and acknowledge who that leader was and then submit to serving the vision of that person.

Working in the film industry had imposed this lesson on us. Like the military, production crews are incredibly hierarchical. It is a very defined leadership pyramid, with the director and producers at the top, the heads of department, senior crew, technicians following and then production assistants, runners and trainees at the bottom. There are clearly defined roles with have their own responsibilities and leadership duties, but there is also a clear pathway for decision-making within the pyramid. Not always is this done well, and people have abused their power far too often in this model, but there is solid logic in this system.

On our first music video shoot together, Genevieve and I had secured permission to film in an aged care facility for the day. An emerging rock band from Genevieve's home town had reached out to ask us to produce their music video to showcase their talent to the world*. Titled *Too Young to Worry*, the premise of the music clip was that the young band members would sneak into an aged care home disguised as elderly residents with grey wigs, slippers and dressing gowns to put on a rock show for the ageing residents. There was a long list of shots we needed to capture, a lot of elderly extras and real residents to wrangle and a film crew to manage. All the while we needed to make sure that we didn't get in the way of the aged care facility functioning as it needed to.

We had often worked together as the producers to organise all of the logistics, but on the day of filming, Genevieve was the director and I the cinematographer. This meant that she was responsible for the overall vision of the clip, leading the performances of the band members and actors, and I was

---

* Technically, one of the band member's mums knew Genevieve's mum and they had been nattering away about what their kids were up to down in the big smoke of Sydney, and said that we should all be working together. Not the coolest of introductions for two young filmmakers trying to be all professional, but working together ensured there were two very proud mothers on the sidelines.

responsible for capturing it in the best way possible with cameras, lighting and the right team. To get a good result, both roles had to collaborate well but also work independently of each other.

We had set ourselves an ambitious challenge to capture everything that we needed in just one day. But with clear roles and responsibilities, we had learnt how to switch from husband and wife to director and cinematographer. Despite the fact that we had probably had a disagreement about something at home that morning, it was crucial for us to be able to serve each other and to allow the other to flourish in their leadership.

The clip was a hit and, as our first music video together, we were proud of the outcome. With the limited production budget, we had even recruited Genevieve's mum to play the role of the angry facility manager and Genevieve's grandma made an appearance as one of the dancing residents!

TAKEAWAYS

Relationships trumps marketing strategies. Connecting with people and forming genuine bonds creates opportunities to understand how we can actually be helpful to them, not sell to them.

Adopt a positive attitude. Even if you don't know how, you can say "yes" and figure it out later. Within reason of course.

Imposter syndrome is natural. But it can be overcome by committing to make the best decisions at the time with the information at hand. If additional information comes along later, you can always change your decision.

CHAPTER NINE | CULTURE

I Once Met Bad Culture: She's a Middle-Aged Film Producer Driving a Porsche Convertible and She Doesn't Give Two Rats About You

So we had made our first hire and work was starting to come to us. One happy client led to another and we were soon being asked to do more and more creative work. To keep up with the demand, we had to start to grow our team to include both freelance creatives and permanent staff to work with us from the studio. We'd been told that the wrong hires can sink a business, so how do you know who are the right people to get on board?

With the choice of either a 'push' or 'pull' mentality, we wanted the right people to be pulled into our orbit of their own volition. I wanted our company to be known for our excellent work and even better culture so that great people would want to be part of what we were doing. We needed to have a great brand.

Now when I say great 'brand' I don't mean a great logo design. You're not alone if you think that a brand is a company's logo, packaging or even the products or services that they sell. These are all a part of the bigger picture but, fundamentally, a company's brand is what people say about them when they have left the room. Here are some common phrases that people say regarding these very well-known brands ...

JUST GOOGLE IT

LET'S NETFLIX AND CHILL TONIGHT

DISNEYLAND IS THE HAPPIEST PLACE ON EARTH

We are pulled into the world of these brands and now talk about them without even realising it, and it's these sort of positive associations that organisations strive for. And when it comes to recruiting, your brand is one of the main reasons people will want to work at your company; it is what you are known for.

For our brand, I focussed on two things: the calibre of work we were creating and the sort of work culture we wanted to have. In the beginning, you need to do any work you can to prove that you can do what you say. But as we started to get a reputation for being friendly people who did great work, we could start to be a little more selective. I had an epiphany during a visit to an animation studio that I greatly admired. They were known for producing some of the best animated TV commercials in the country and I was keen to find out their secret. As I walked through their studios with their General Manager, I was impressed by framed print after framed print lining the hallways, showcasing the amazing campaigns and films that they had created. And it hit me: one great project leads to the next. I wrote down the simple formula as soon as I left the building ...

DO GREAT WORK

↓

TELL PEOPLE ABOUT IT

↓

THEY WANT YOU TO DO GREAT WORK FOR THEM

↓

DO MORE GREAT WORK

[RINSE + REPEAT]

In the early days of working on TV commercials, one afternoon I was particularly tired as we approached the end of the final day of a three-day shoot for raisin toast. Really not very exciting stuff. And my lack of enthusiasm must have shown as the head of the camera department caught my eye, leant over and whispered with a smile, 'You're only as good as your last job.' She was reminding me that if you do great work, you're more likely to be able to do more great work.

It certainly wasn't rocket science, but we've stuck to the formula and it's worked. And then, to ensure that we created a work culture that great people would want to be a part of, we worked on an equally simple formula: there's twenty-four hours in a day. If an employee works a standard eight-hour day, and is getting the recommended eight hours sleep each night, once you take out lunchbreaks and transit time, that employee will spend more of their waking hours with the people at work than they will with their loved ones. Viewed through a mortal lens, we each only get a limited number of days on this planet, so our theory was simple: ensure that those eight hours at work are the best that they can be. We wanted people to want to come to work.

Working on a variety of feature films, I had seen the impact of different work cultures on a team. Fortunately, most films provided great environments to work in. But on one, the culture was absolutely awful. A spirit of fear and intimidation had been seeded from the top by the director and producer which meant it was a horrible place to go to work each day. They were both out to prove themselves and didn't care how many people they had to step on to get there.

It wasn't a particularly large budget production and with no paid role openings, I had volunteered to work in the camera department and was quickly 'promoted'* to the position of second assistant camera (2nd AC). I'm not an advocate of productions exploiting volunteers, particularly for more than a few days without some sort of compensation. The producer of this project was not a particularly pleasant person and so she had jumped at the opportunity of free labour. A few weeks into production some of my senior colleagues even went to her to advocate that I should get paid at least a minimal wage, but she refused outright.

---

* Promoted, but no change to my $0 salary.

For four weeks we were filming at a beach-side property, a two-and-a-half-hour drive from my house in the Adelaide Hills. The producer, being a selfish woman, had refused to pay for accommodation for the crew so everyone had had to drive there and back each day. I'm pretty sure it's illegal now, but it made for extremely long working days. She herself decided that it was too far for her to drive, so she only came out and visited the set twice during the whole four weeks. I ended up moving into a friend's house on the other side of town for a month, purely to cut out an hour of driving each way.

The epitome of the production's bad culture came one morning on set. It was a freezing cold June morning, we had been up since 3.30 am to get to set before sunrise, and crew morale was particularly low. Of all of the days, this was the day that the producer had decided to come and visit the set. When the crew is tired and the mood is low, this is a great opportunity for the production's leadership to step in and boost everyone's spirits with some encouragement. Our producer? Yeah ... nah.

I vividly remember her driving onto set in her Porsche convertible with a scarf wrapped around her neck and a takeaway coffee in hand. Without even getting out of her car, she took one look around and said, 'Looks like a cold one' and then drove straight back to Adelaide. Her obnoxious and uncaring attitude seeped through the entire production, resulting in a team that had no motivation for excellence and no reason to do any more than the bare minimum. By the end of the film's nine-week shoot, the crew were rundown and despondent and I was glad to be leaving the project*. It's no surprise that the resulting film flopped. You can always feel when a project has been created with love and care—two things that the culture on this project certainly lacked.

Fast forward a few years to running our own productions and I knew without any doubt the impact a positive or negative culture could have, not just on a team but also on the quality of their work. So even if it's as small as a celebratory meat pie or a fresh coconut, we deliberately magnified the importance of celebrating people.

After one family visit back to Adelaide, I returned home to Sydney with a large rainbow decoration that my parents used to hang up for our birthdays each year when we were kids.

---

* Still unpaid.

Known affectionately as 'the birthday ball', each time it was hung up we knew a celebration was imminent. As we were no longer kids and had all moved out of home, the birthday ball had lain dormant in a bottom drawer so I thought it could be fun to share it with our team back in the studio. Despite the fact that we were a team of fully-grown adults, our staff loved it. On each of their birthdays, we would hang the birthday ball above their chair and decorate their desk with balloons and streamers. It was a chance to be kids again and an invitation to revel in that childlike joy.

Another source of pure joy was our Taste Christmas parties: always a highlight in my diary. They were an opportunity to celebrate our staff and freelance crew and to involve their families in our journey. Being a big fan of the TV series *The Office**, one year I introduced my own version of Michael Scott's staff awards night, 'The Dundies'. So, at our Christmas party, with everyone dressed in the most garish Christmas sweaters that we could find, I brought forward 'The Tasties' and revealed a collection of mismatched hand-made trophies. Being thrifty, I had decided to make unique trophies for each

---

* I'm a big fan of both the UK and US versions. If you have a spare four hours and want a full analytic review or a total Office nerd out, give me a call. But for the sake of this story, I'm referring to the fabulous Steve Carell's character from the US version.

staff member, each symbolising the spirit of their award: plastic dinosaurs, juggling balls, wooden hamburgers and coloured figurines were all glued onto wooden bases and spray-painted gold.

Each year the number and complexity of awards increased as our invite list expanded to include our suppliers, partner companies, board members and advisers. It got to a point that I had to start sourcing all of the individual trophy items a good two months prior to the event and our small inner-city courtyard would get covered in plastic sheeting so I could spray-paint the dozens of awards.

My intentions were for a bit of fun and camaraderie: a novel way to individually acknowledge and thank each staff member to ensure that everyone knew that their hard work had been seen and that they were highly valued. It wasn't until years later when the Covid-19 pandemic hit that I realised just how much these awards had meant to people. As the whole world started working from home, I was touched to see many Tasty awards displayed with great pride in the background of our colleagues' video calls. Being seen and acknowledged had meant so much to each of them and continued to foster a place of belonging.

Another wonderful event during the year was our annual company retreat. It was always a great opportunity to deepen our culture, strengthen teamwork, and review the everyday operations of the business. I would book a large house a few hours out of Sydney along the coast and take our team away for two nights. It was important to get out of our day-to-day neighbourhood to encourage staff to switch off from their everyday work mode and switch into a 'big picture' mindset to look outwardly at our impact and inwardly at how we function.

While I had scheduled time in the agenda to work on recalibrating our trajectory towards our company vision and refining our production processes, the main priority was for the team to bond. We would cook meals together, swim at the beach and play fiercely competitive games of *Lord of the Rings Monopoly* late into the night, with the movie's soundtrack blaring in the background of course! And I would always work in a competitive challenge to try and encourage the team outside of their comfort zone.

One year this happened to be a high ropes course. Up in the trees, the team would need to manoeuvre from tree to tree across zip lines, ladders and rope bridges to get across the finish line. But as we arrived, we were greeted by an empty car park and quickly deduced why we were the only group there. Billowing winds had the tree tops swaying violently from side to side and all of the other visitors had sensibly abandoned their adventure plans. Our climbing guide came marching out to meet us with a big smile on his face. 'Ready to go?' he beamed, unperturbed by the anxious looks on all of our faces, 'There's a bit of a breeze, but she'll be right!'

Thirty minutes later we were harnessed in tightly and clinging to the tree trunks as we swayed in the wind. With looks of sheer terror, high up in the treetops, we made our way from obstacle to obstacle. Any thought of a race to the finish line had completely vanished. Team members were hoisting each other over suspended cargo nets, supporting each other across rope swings and cheering one another on to overcome mental and physical hurdles. The sense of achievement as the last person abseiled off the final wooden platform was palpable. Years later, the team would still be talking about this adventure with great fondness. Together we had conquered something that, alone, many of us wouldn't have even thought of trying.

TAKEAWAYS

Your brand is what people way about you when you have left the room. It is the positive (or negative) association with how you are perceived, and is a key reason people will or will not want to work with you.

Make your business a place that people want to work at. Knowing that they will spend more awake hours at work than they will with their loved ones, we as leaders have an obligation to ensure it is the best place possible.

Magnify the importance of celebrating others. The value of being seen and acknowledged cannot be underestimated.

CHAPTER TEN | **PEOPLE**

Art Is a Team Sport

With our two simple theories to attract great people in action, we started to see specific types of people coming into our orbit. Filmmakers and creatives with very high-calibre artistry had seen our work and wanted to collaborate—creative agency producers who had heard about our work ethic and wanted to be a part of a team that cared about lifestyle balance, and executives who had seen our impact on inclusion and diversity and wanted to be a part of a company that advocated and created opportunities for marginalised people.

So, as we grew, we didn't have to scout far to find great people who were aligned with our mission because many of them found us. We had also found that recruiting from within the networks of our own people was very beneficial. People with values, talent and good work ethic usually build their friendship circles with people similar to them.

One particular hire came out of nowhere. A young woman called Viv had seen our work and heard all about our inclusive filmmaking and so she wanted in. We didn't have any open roles or opportunities but she was so passionate that she turned up anyway. Viv's enthusiasm was infectious and she quickly realised that she had found a group of like-minded people, so she latched on tightly. Viv looked around and noticed that we weren't particularly active on social media, just the occasional post on the company Facebook or Instagram when we remembered. So she piped up and said, 'Why don't I help with your social media? I'll do it in my own time!' It was a hard proposition to argue with. So the next day Viv returned and began volunteering two days a week to help us plan out and create content for socials, rather than just posting whatever popped into our minds. I knew exactly what was happening: she was creating a space just her size.

Sure enough, within two weeks Viv had created a space just for her. She was such a positive influence and had become a wonderful addition to our team that we created a permanent role for her without hesitation.

Unfortunately, it wasn't as clear cut when I needed to fire my first staff member. In the early days of our business, I thought that our company would be a place where anyone could work. We wouldn't be exclusive and our doors were open to everyone. But I was very wrong. It's certainly not that we were exclusive, but I had to learn that only a certain calibre of person had the right makeup to help us further our vision.

Of course the mantra is to 'hire slow, fire fast' which I was completely onboard with ... in principle. We had been very considerate and took our time with the hiring, and when such a time came that I would need to let someone go, I was sure I would do it quickly. Rip off the Band-Aid. The problem was that when the time did come, I convinced myself that I didn't need to fire this staff member. He had had some family issues at home. We had banded around him to do all we could to help. But weeks later he was still coming in late without notice, had a snappy attitude with his colleagues, was being short with clients and at times even became insubordinate.

I told myself that he just needed more support, more help, more training, more adjustments. I was determined to do everything I could to help him get back on track and succeed. I gave him extra time off, I ignored the bad attitude and I didn't pull him up when his work was sloppy. In retrospect, these are exceptionally clear warning signs, but I saw it as my own failing if someone didn't work out at our company.

For over nine months* I tolerated his sub-par performance and even worse attitude. Each week, I would offload complaints to Brian, my business coach, and then, in the same breath, defend against his sound advice that I had done all I could and I now needed to terminate the employee. I watched on as the rest of the team bore the brunt of this underperforming team member and they would often fall into the firing line of his bad attitude. I felt terrible knowing that my team was being burdened by my lack of action.

At the end of nine very long months, the lacklustre staff member's contract came to an end. As his final day came to a close, he packed up his things, smiled at the door and muttered

---

* I know, nine months! I can feel your sharp inhalation at my lack of action.

'Ok, thanks' as he left the studio for the last time. I smiled and waved politely, but on the inside I was ready to collapse in a heap, exhausted from trying to do everything but terminate him. I had just concluded a nine-month masterclass in discerning whether someone is the right fit or not, and understanding the consequences of not acting more quickly.

After this lesson, I started looking for two main qualities in people when recruiting: aptitude and attitude. I had discovered that a skillset can be taught, but you can't teach attitude. We were looking for people who shone under pressure. Not because our workplace was always under high pressure, but because it is under pressure that people's true attitudes come out. I adjusted my focus slightly and began actively looking for people who would still be buoyant and optimistic if we had to pull an all-nighter to hit a deadline, or people who could empathise with a client after they requested a revision to a project schedule for the twentieth time, or people who would have a smile on their face at 5 am in the middle of a damp field as we shivered in the cold, waiting to film a sunrise.

Everyone had to be an all-round A-grade player. A-grade players are not only excellent in their chosen field, but they are excellent at working with their teammates, highly teachable and are great teachers themselves, able to bring others up to their level. But the thing about A-grade players is that they want to work with other A-grade players. They will either seek out others who operate at their level, or raise up those around them to their level. So my recruitment posture shifted to protecting the A-grade players already on my team and I became more selective about who I was willing to bring into the team with them. When you allow a B-grade or C-grade player onto the field, particularly one without the ability or attitude to want to become an A-grade player, the whole team loses momentum as they work doubly hard to carry the lesser player.

Our recruitment was not just limited to our permanent staff of course; it included our team of suppliers. From film crew and technicians to printers, IT, strategists, tax accountants and lawyers, we worked hard to ensure that all the people we worked with were aligned to our values and purpose, and were not just sufficient suppliers. I remember as I gave my speech at the launch of *I Didn't Like Hubert*, I glanced over and saw our tax accountant sitting in the front row. He is incredibly talented at what he does and is a sought-after and busy man, but here he was, beaming his big smile, just as he did when he had come to all of our events in the past. He has never missed one of our project launches or film premieres. These were the sorts of people that we tried to surround ourselves with. We nicknamed them our 'Taste Folk'.

When it came to creating a culture that cared about people, one tool to understand how people work best that I found extremely useful was behavioural profiling. It's a common tool for businesses and I had trialled different corporate personality tests since starting our own business. But it wasn't until some entrepreneurial friends told me about a platform that they had been using with great effect that I found a system that worked really well for us*. The system was structured to uncover a person's _natural_ behaviour and then showcase how they work effectively with other people. We can all pretend to be whoever we want to be when we're in an easy, relaxed environment, but as soon as we are under pressure (which we all are at different times) then that's when our natural behaviours will always come out.

---

*   For those interested, or if you're just a big psychology geek, google 'Brilliant Fit DNA Behaviour'. Not a paid promotion, although Malcolm if you're reading this, I'll send you my bank details. Totally joking.

Rather than just being an insightful management tool, this became a secret weapon for fast-tracking team development. The system would display each person's natural inclination on a spectrum in comparison to the rest of society. I started using the profiles regularly with our staff in team-building sessions and we would work to understand how each of us naturally functioned under pressure. I was frequently seeing the 'Aha' moments in my colleagues' eyes as they uncovered crucial insights about their teammates and understood why they preferred to work a certain way.

For fun, I would pull out a number of behavioural traits from my own reports with the team and unpack how they came through in my work. I am naturally very comfortable initiating new things: I'm risk tolerant and original in my thinking (a couple of the traits you may come to expect from an entrepreneur). You could see this in me even as a young kid when I grew bored with my finished tree houses and wanted to go build another.

Understanding these traits allowed me to quickly see my blind spots: attention to detail, risk assessment and the interest to see things through. So when I am working on a project, I either need to be extra aware of these weaknesses, or try to work with someone who naturally possesses these skills and can complement me. And as soon as the two of us knew each other well and understood the strengths that we each brought to the table, we could fast-track our ability to work well together as a team.

These profiles also became a useful tool for communicating with each other. Particularly when helping to get a dysfunctional team back on track or resolving a conflict; having the insights into how a person naturally works when under pressure was so helpful. I could adapt my behaviour and language to suit the person, even down to the type of settings where we chose to have a meeting. For some staff, I knew it was best to situate ourselves in a relaxed environment, usually sitting next to each other on a couch or outside at the cafe next door to our office and starting the conversation with genuine interest in their world before softly transitioning into the work discussion. Other people, like myself, preferred to be more direct and get to the point quickly. I would sit opposite them at a table or talk candidly while we walked to a meeting and brush quickly through any small talk to be able to lay out the situation in frank, unfiltered terms.

These tools gave us incredible insights into each other and a much deeper understanding of how to get the best results when we worked together.

More often than not, team members came into our world in conventional ways: applying for a role, interviewing, being offered a role and seeing out a trial period. But one particular team member almost fell into our world. Javed was an up-and-coming creative a mutual friend had recommended come in and say hello. Having recently moved to the big smoke in Sydney from a regional town up on the coast, he had been hopping from job to job to make ends meet while doing some animation and editing work on the side. With no formal creative training or any experience working in a production company, he was not the most usual candidate. But he was highly teachable, ooze with talent and showed great potential. Aptitude and attitude: tick.

Like when Viv came to us, we didn't have any open roles or any projects that we needed freelancers on, but Javed asked if he could hire a desk from us so he could have a creative space to come and work from each day. An easy yes. He moved his small edit setup the next day and settled right in. Naturally just by being around, we would all share what we were working on.

And in no time at all, I was asking him if he could help me out on odd jobs: compose a bit of music here, animate a title there. Without realising it, Javed was also beginning to make a space just his size. Mirroring Wendy's earlier rental deal with us, we proposed that Javed work for us for four hours a week in lieu of paying rent for his desk. But we were so blown away by his talent and attitude that after just a couple of weeks we offered him a permanent role with us, even though we didn't have a job for him straight away.

It wasn't until we were away filming a music video that I saw Javed's true character emerge. Members of Australian folk band Tigertown knew Javed well and were keen for him to direct their next music video. Not knowing how to produce a project like this, Javed brought the project in-house and we were excited to bring the video to life. But we needed a concept that could be created on a small budget, as was very typical with music clips. The track was called 'Morning Has Finally Come' and Javed had some great ideas about a group of people who carry the sun across the countryside at night and set it afloat atop a hill, creating a sunrise each morning. We thought it was a lovely concept and so set about working out how on earth we were going to make it happen.

We allocated nearly our entire budget to hiring a 1.5 metre wide inflatable light up ball* and a generator to run it from and then convinced a friend to lend us his holiday house on a remote property to film for a few days. Five hours south of Sydney, we set up camp at the homestead on the Snowy River and then quickly realised our terrible error.... We were planning to shoot outside through the night for the next couple of evenings and it was smack bang in the middle of winter. To make matters worse, the house was at the bottom of a valley below the Snowy Mountains, which, as the name suggests, are pretty cold mountain ranges. When the breeze picked up, icy wind blew directly from the snow-capped mountains straight down the gully and onto us. Luckily, we all had our eyes fixed firmly on the same vision and we were determined to pull this off.

Each night, as the sun would go down, we rugged up in every jumper and jacket we could lay our hands on, clambered across riverbeds and trekked up hillsides, capturing beautiful imagery of a troupe carrying this giant glowing ball across the countryside. The camaraderie of the cast and crew was

---

* These lights were designed to be used on film sets as giant sources of soft light, often for filming large outdoor night scenes. So you can imagine the surprise of the hire company when we said we wanted a bunch of people to carry the ball across a paddock and then hoist it up into the sky at sunrise.

incredible, certainly not something that one person could pull off on their own. The pastor at our old church in the city used to say, 'The maturity of leadership is not getting people to go where you want, but allowing others to take you.' I was watching this unfold before my eyes, and it was lovely to behold.

For the finale of the clip, once the band had hoisted the light up into the sky at dawn, we needed a big wide shot of an actual sunrise to see the spectacle of the new day illuminating the Australian landscape. Unfortunately, each evening as we worked through until dawn, the sunrises were overcast and grey. By our final evening before we were due to return to Sydney the next day, we knew we only had one chance left. We had captured everything else we needed, we just required our majestic sunrise.

We sat around the fire that evening and checked the weather radar for the thousandth time, praying for a clear forecast. Nothing but rain for the next twenty-four hours. We had no choice but to finish the music video without our grand finale, and so the team retired to their beds downtrodden. But Javed, ever the optimist, coerced me into agreeing to get up and trek to the top of the hill with our cameras. Just in case. As my 4 am alarm went off, I immediately knew we had no chance.

Rain was pounding loudly on the tin roof above; we would be drenched to the bone as soon as we stepped outside and our equipment would be saturated in seconds. I gave in to fate and went back asleep.

But an hour later, I was awoken by a tentative knock at my door and there stood Javed in the semi-darkness, a giant smile on his face. 'The rain's easing!' he beamed. He'd sat awake since 4 am and listened to the rain on the galvanised roof, hoping for a break. And finally it had come.

We threw our warmest clothes back on, bundled up our film equipment and clambered into the old ute we'd hired for the week. It was still dark but dawn was only minutes away. Having shot plenty of sunrises in my time, I knew we were racing against the clock. Whether you're ready with the cameras or not, the sun will always rise! So we tore up the road in the darkness, our path barely visible with the weak headlights. After several minutes, we pulled off the road and onto a dirt track that would lead us up to the top of the hill. But as we made the turn, the car slid from side to side. After all the rain throughout the night, the dirt track was a washout, and no matter how hard we tried, the tyres couldn't get a grip on the track. There was no way we were going to be able to drive up the track.

Without missing a beat, Javed jumped out of the ute, bundled up our gear and headed up the track towards the top of the hill. Undertaking a half march, half run, we climbed the final kilometre and made it to the summit with seconds to spare. Panting and exhausted from our early morning Tough Mudder practice run, we quickly set up our cameras and rolled on a spectacular sunrise that painted the countryside with gorgeous hues of orange, pinks and purples.

Masters of collaboration, the team from Pixar call art a team sport. I had just witnessed the result of a team of aligned and motivated artists all pulling in the same direction and it was magnificent. Teamwork really did make the dream work.

TAKEAWAYS

Recruit from within your network. People with values, talent and good work ethic usually build their friendship circles with people similar to them.

Don't ignore the warning signs. When you see repeated bad behaviour or attitude and they are not willing to course correct, fire fast.

Hire people based on attitude. The rest can be taught, but nine times out of ten attitude can not.

A-grade players want to play with A-grade players. They will either seek out those that operate at their level or raise up others around them to their level. Failing that, they will leave.

Behaviour profiling helps to understand how we work under pressure. Behaviour profiles identify blind spots and fast-track team development. Using team profiles help to understand how to best communicate and work with each other is a game changer.

CHAPTER ELEVEN | **VALUES**

I Knew We Were Doing Something Right When a Colleague Called Me Out

Do you ever drive around and see service trucks with their company logo splashed on the side and their values emblazoned beneath? It's usually something like 'Integrity', 'Honesty' and 'Quality'. Or have you walked into a corporate office and found yourself face to face with its company values printed in large glossy letters above the reception desk? Probably words like, 'Trust', 'Reliability' and 'Value'.

It's not that I don't like company values or glossy words printed on walls, but integrity, reliability, quality, [insert generic positive word here] aren't values. These are basic human qualities that we should all possess as a foundational starting point. We shouldn't need to brag that our business has these basics down pat. Sadly that's not the case—there are plenty of businesses out there run by the dodgy brothers, so I'm sure the word 'reliability' advertised alongside the local plumber would be a very welcome sign to a trauma-induced customer of a nightmare plumber. But we can do better!

Meaningful company values serve two important purposes: they are an invitation for people to become a part of why the company exists and they are a navigation aid when we find ourselves in a challenging situation. The queen of vulnerability, Brené Brown, shared on her podcast: 'When the waters are deep and swift and I am in a hard place, my values are the most consistent life raft for me.' Providing critical guiding parameters, our values enable us as a team to determine the right courses of action, rather than leaving this just to the business owners each time.

On our annual retreats, a key focus is to zero in on our company values. Early on in our journey, we worked to establish these values together, pinpointing words and phrases that articulated what was most important to us. Together, we agreed that our values would determine the type of people and organisations that we would work with, how we would work with each other, and the behaviours and attitudes that we would hold each other accountable to. To help us uncover more meaningful values we would think about particular moments where a colleague had shone through—a moment that reflected the best side of the organisation. We each went away and came back with an eclectic list of moments from our company's history. As we shared, we heard about grandiose moments that had shaped the course of the company as well as tiny little actions that were seemingly insignificant to most of us but had made a big impact on someone.

To kick off the discussions, I excitedly shared a quality I had observed in Javed time and time again. By now our longest-standing employee, he had never presented a project that was just 'good'. Everything he worked on was 'great'. Often this would mean that his deadlines were missed because he had stayed up all night working on the animation of a character's jump, or finding the perfect piece of music for a film's edit*. But Javed would not stop searching until he found the greatness in every project he was on and he never submitted a piece of work until it was great, and here lay our first value: 'Make it great!'

---

* I subsequently learnt to schedule in extra time on the jobs Javed was on, just in case.

In everything we work on, how we treat each other and in all that we do, make it great.

After a 'fill your heart with pride' team session sharing these wonderful observed moments, our suite of values emerged and we had a wholistic reflection of who we were:

1. Nourishing Content Only
   We create content that helps to make the world a better place

2. Curious Learners
   In everything we do we are curious, teachable and open

3. Nothing But the Best
   We only put the best that we can do out into the world

4. Yes People
   We are always willing problem solvers, starting with the "yes" and working backwards from there

5. 100% Inclusive
   We create opportunities for people living with disability to thrive in front and behind the camera, as well as advocating for inclusion through our work

Our values became our unmoveable principles of who we are, what we do, how we work and most importantly, why we do it. In our Taste Handbook, a handy guide for new staff when joining our team, I proudly display on the opening pages:

> OUR VALUES PENETRATE DEEPER
> THAN WORDS PRINTED ON A WALL
> OUR VALUES ARE OUR <u>NORTHERN STAR</u>

Between annual retreats, it took plenty of repetition to keep our values top of mind; however, I knew our values had cemented in when I'd overhear our staff holding each other accountable to them. But as the captain of the ship, I didn't expect that it would be one of my own employees who would need to hold me accountable.

Late one afternoon I was standing on the docks of the Brisbane cruise passenger terminal, having just returned from five days of filming on a cruise ship. Shooting on location, particularly jobs that take us away to interesting locations, are always a lot of fun, so the production team with me was in great spirits. Unfortunately, cruise ships are notorious for having no phone reception and very patchy WI-FI while out at sea. So, after we had hauled all of our equipment off the ship, our phones began to ping with dozens of messages and emails from the team back in the studio.

My good mood quickly turned south when I saw multiple urgent emails from one of our clients, alerting me that something had gone awry on another project in production. It appeared that one of the team members had overlooked a crucial detail and hence the project had been delayed and the deadline had been missed. Not an irreparable situation, but I personally took particular pride in always delivering our projects on time. Or, at the least, ensuring the client knew well in advance if something hadn't gone to plan.

Well, the deadline was missed, the client hadn't been informed, and now they wanted an explanation. From me. Right now. Needless to say, I wasn't impressed. I quickly scrambled to find out what was going on. As I went through the backlog of emails, a montage of moments when team members had dropped the ball in the past, not communicated what was going on, or tried to cut a corner to save time flashed across my mind. I was convinced that without me there to manage the project myself, the wheels had completely come off. I called Bree, my Head of Production back in the studio, looking for some answers.

But before she could get a word in to explain, I found myself rattling off a list of established procedures, expectations of creative excellence and the importance of proactive communication. Bree copped an earful from me before promising to find out the latest on the project and then to call me back with an update.

As I waited, I paced around the terminal and felt the cool ocean breeze starting to lower my frustration levels. Fifteen minutes later, my phone rang and Bree's even-tempered voice greeted me with an answer I hadn't expected. She had known exactly what was happening on the project when I had called before, but had decided to take a minute to compose herself. 'One of our values is that we treat each other with care and we trust each other,' Bree recited to me, in a half statement, half question. I was caught off guard. She patiently explained the project situation, that something had indeed been missed but the team had stayed late the previous evening and come in early that morning to rectify the error. The client had been informed, but that hadn't gotten through to their team when the senior project leader had left me the latest message.

I felt foolish. I hadn't taken the time to find out the whole picture and I hadn't put my own team first. Not first ahead of the client, but first as human beings. For years, I had said to the team that, at Taste, first you are a person: a person with feelings and needs and talents and a life outside of work. And then, second, you are a collaborator: a director, a writer, a bookkeeper, a designer. But in this moment, I had completely forgotten to see my own team as people first. I had skipped straight past finding out what was happening back at the studio, forgetting that as human beings, they are a group of talented, hard-working and trustworthy people. In this moment I was embarrassed, but I was also delighted; our values had infused to such a level that a team member was willing to stand up to the boss for the values of our own company.

After this important interaction, channelling behaviour and decisions through our values was a no-brainer. When we find ourselves in difficult situations, the right answer nearly always presents itself when we sift it through our values. Not only do I personally find it helpful in my own decision-making, but it takes the pressure off me. When staff come looking for answers, I spin it around and empower them to find the right solution. Our values empower every staff member to be able to make great decisions with the best interests of our company, our clients and each other, every time.

TAKEAWAYS

Company values are not just wall decorations. Meaningful values invite people to become a part of why the company exists and serve as a navigation aid when we find ourselves in challenging situations.

Engraining values takes repetition. But you will know you've repeated yourself enough when you overhear staff holding each other accountable to them.

CHAPTER TWELVE | SUPPORTING THE TEAM
Learning How to Get the Eggs

IF YOU WANT TO GO FAST → GO ALONE.

IF YOU WANT TO GO <u>FAR</u> ⟶ <u>GO TOGETHER</u>.

I don't remember when I first heard this pearl of wisdom, but this African proverb has stuck with me for a very long time. The 'going together' was exactly what I had been seeking ever since I had made my stop-motion film *Larry* all by myself. I may have been moving fast and I never had to argue with anyone about my creative ideas but, at the end of the day, I was alone. Even at just fifteen, I knew that I wanted to build a team that I could collaborate with.

But I had to learn a few basic lessons first ...

I've always struggled with control. I never thought of myself as a 'controlling' person, but being vulnerable here for a minute, I like things to be done a certain way. The day that Brian, my coach, gently challenged me on the notion of control, I was almost offended. I had always considered myself a very open, collaborative and supportive person to work with. But I eventually realised* that I was happy to go with the flow, so long as the direction of said flow was towards the destination I intended to reach. So yeah, pretty controlling.

From my early years in primary school, I developed a dread of group assignments. I always seemed to get partnered with someone who wouldn't pull their weight. I'm sure the teachers didn't do it on purpose, but it used to drive me crazy. I would want to start early on the project and plan out who's doing what, and they would usually be more than happy to just sit back, relax and, in the end, leave it all up to me. And because we were being graded together, I would panic and put lots of work into the

---

* Less my realisation, and more that Brian continuously shone an uncomfortably bright light on my blind spot until I was ready to embrace it.

project to make sure we (rather, I) did well. Now that I look back on it, learning how to work with difficult people, or even just people who are different to us, may have been the crux of the teacher's assignment all along.

Running a business, I had to learn how to manage this need for control. Naturally, being my own business, there is a requirement for me to control things to a certain extent: the need to pay our debts, duty of care, ensure we operate within the law, lodge our taxes. All the fun bits. But, for the majority of times, I needed to give over control and empower others to do the bits that they were really good at.

When it came to managing people, I tried to compensate for my controlling tendencies and started to go too far the other way. Mentors would regularly remind me to 'scrutinise the process, not the person, meaning make sure the process works first. I thought I was empowering people by setting the task and letting them figure it all out by themselves. And sometimes I wouldn't even be super clear on the task, so as not to be too prescriptive. I figured that they were smart, creative and independent people who didn't want to be micromanaged.

The problem was, if you ask a hard-working person to get to work on a task with few or no parameters, they will. But nine times out of ten, the end result won't be what I needed them to do in the first place. The task would likely get done, but it would be over budget, have missed the deadline or not fulfil the brief at all. I wasn't doing them or myself any favours.

Instead, I had to discover how to become really clear on what the task was and outline the steps and expectations to complete the task. The trick to not controlling the situation was then to create space for input. I would outline the task and steps and then say, 'What do you think?' or 'How do you feel about this?' This would often catch people off guard, but it created an opportunity for their buy-in and ownership. It created a language of value and equality that said I wanted their input. In doing this, I may need to spend plenty of time affirming and redirecting their ideas to align back with the task but, so often, great ideas and insights would emerge that I hadn't thought of. And it would be these projects that I am most proud of because when I look at the finished result, I don't see a reflection of my own ideas and abilities, but the work and input of a really clever team.

I also had to learn how to sustain our staff when times were very busy, and determine what simple things we could do to ensure our team had everything it needed to succeed. One ordinary Friday afternoon I sat down with Bree, as we always did at the end of the week, to look through our upcoming production workload. Before we had even begun, we knew we were going to be extremely busy for the next couple of months because we had run out of clipboards. Let me explain …

At one end of our studio, we had created a giant production wall. It was literally that: a wall displaying every project that was currently in production. For years, we had tried and tested many project management programs available to keep on top of our jobs in production, but we had never found a system that gelled. So we decided to make our own. But as none of us had the skills to create our own software, we opted to just make it in real life. We constructed three 10 foot high timber panels mounted to the wall with numerous metal rails running from side to side. Each rail was identified as a stage in production and then, hanging on the rails, was a small clipboard with all of a project's details on display. Standing back from the wall, we could easily see how many projects were in scripting, how many were out shooting, or in which version of an edit they were in. It was a great way to visually forecast where the pressure points might occur weeks before it would actually happen.

On this Friday afternoon as we looked over our production wall, every single stage of production was full up with clipboards and we had just won a couple of large new projects that needed to be added to the mix. The pressure was about to be turned up. Bree and I looked at each other with nervous but excited expressions, and I made a mental note that we needed to buy some more clipboards. And maybe create a bigger production wall.

In this approaching busy season, my role as the leader was not going to be constantly out the front steering the way, but sustaining the team to make it through this upcoming sprint. I like the image of a shepherd with their flock of sheep; they move between leading out the front where they navigate and clear the path for the flock, but then spend a lot of time going back through the pack to ensure that each was keeping up and none were getting left behind. We had a very capable and clever team, but they were going to need plenty of encouragement to make it through this busy period and we needed to ensure that they weren't taken out by any obstacles if we could avoid it.

In the midst of a bushfire season, no matter how many fires are blazing, it is critical to always keep someone up in the watchtower looking out for small spot fires that can start without warning. If caught early, a team can be deployed to deal with it quickly. But if left unattended, the results can be devastating. So, I repositioned Bree high up in a metaphorical watchtower with a good view over all of our projects, taking her hands off the day-to-day production tasks and allowing her to watch over all of our projects, with a sharp eye looking out for spot fires. My job then became supporting her to stay up there for as long as possible. Our daily catchups became focussed around what potential hurdles could be, putting out any spot fires and determining what we could do to clear the paths so our team could charge ahead*.

A few years later, I was the executive producer on a short-form TV series we were creating. Different from producing,

---

* I may have mixed in too many metaphors here: sheep, spot fires, hurdles. But I'm sure you get the drift!

an executive producer is much more hands off from the daily production of the show, but responsible for the overall direction, creation and delivery of the project. I had been so used to directing and producing where I was knee-deep in creative ideas and making things come to life, that this was quite a different role to take on. My wife, Genevieve, was the series creator, so I knew we were in safe hands, but I still had to fight the urge to jump in and take the reins on plenty of occasions.

Guiding the team through to ensure we achieved great results and navigating all of the challenges that come with such a production was no small task. Once again I had to quickly learn what my role as a leader looked like in this situation, and how we could achieve the outcomes we needed, without taking over the project myself.

Many times throughout this project I was reminded of one of my favourite parables. Its origins aren't as noble as that of a biblical parable, but instead comedic legend Lorne Michaels came up with it. Readers may not know this name, but will likely be familiar with the people he has played a large part in helping to establish. Lorne created the late-night comedy show *Saturday Night Live* (*SNL*) in 1975 and has served as the showrunner for nearly every season since its inception to now. Many of the greatest modern-day American comedians and performers got their big breaks at SNL including Will Ferrell, Eddie Murphy, Tina Fey, Adam Sandler, Chevy Chase, Steve Carell, Amy Poehler, Mike Myers, Bill Murray, Kristen Wiig and Steve Martin, just to name a few.

In Tina Fey's biography Bossypants, she recalls a story Lorne would often recite which I have since shared with many aspiring leaders;

A MAN GOES TO A PSYCHIATRIST AND SAYS,
MY BROTHER'S GONE CRAZY. HE THINKS HE'S A CHICKEN.

AND THE PSYCHIATRIST SAYS,
HAVE YOU TOLD HIM HE'S NOT A CHICKEN?

THE MAN REPLIES,
I WOULD BUT WE NEED THE EGGS.

As leaders, we all need to know how to get the eggs—the ability to stand back and let people share ideas, express emotions, debate approaches and put it all out on the table (particularly when working with people from younger generations).

And then be able to say, 'Ok, I hear that. I've taken it all onboard and here's what we're going to do …'

There are times too many to count when I've tried to lead a group of people who appear to be running off in multiple directions and had to remind myself that I'm not here to be a dictator, nor to be the star of the show. I'm here to get the eggs.

TAKEAWAYS

Give over control. By becoming clear on the task and outlining the expectations, we empower those around us. But even more beneficial, when we create space for their input, opportunity for buy-in and ownership is formed.

When times are busy, sustain the person up in the watchtower. They need to be able to stay up there to identify any spot fires so the team can act quickly when needed.

CHAPTER THIRTEEN | BALANCE
A Jar of Rocks Changed My Life

Just because you're led by purpose, doesn't mean the journey is going to be smooth sailing. Within three years, our team of three had expanded to eight talented creatives who could write, direct, design, animate, produce and edit films. From the outside, things were looking impressive, but on the inside, we were facing some challenges.

Obtaining new business was clunky and irregular and we were fearful of falling into the cycle of 'feeding the beast'*. As we were more of a boutique production company, it was

---

* Feeding the beast: when a team scales to match the demand of work, but soon after a continuous stream of work is required to be able keep all of those people busy and pay for all of their salaries.

difficult to know who to target to advertise our services, but we had began discovering that 'Diversity and Inclusion' (D&I) was becoming a much bigger focus for corporate workplaces, with many creating new roles to specifically focus on increasing the diversity of staff recruits and ensure employees felt included in the workforce. Our work with inclusive filmmaking was a natural fit to help organisations not just talk the talk, but walk the walk in producing their D&I messaging to cover people from marginalised backgrounds.

We were also discovering that it didn't matter how clever our business development plans might be: the best opportunities were coming out of organic relationships. One of those fortuitous crossing of paths happened at an industry dinner. A woman named Diane sat down next to Genevieve and naturally they began talking about what they both did. It turned out that Diane was the Diversity and Inclusion Manager at Australia Post, Australia's national postal service. They had a workforce of over 40,000 people spread out across the country who they wanted to engage with the importance of D&I, and so she asked if we could possibly help.

For most ordinary workplaces this is a difficult requirement. Authentic and successful D&I is not a corporate value or mandate, but is most effective when embraced and embodied by the management and staff. The challenge is that most staff want to be left to perform the job they were hired for and so any messaging or additional requests from the corporate head office often felt burdensome or a time-wasting distraction.

Instead of pumping out more corporate communications that told people why D&I is important, we applied our inclusive methodology and turned to engaging the staff in the process, fundamentally dictating the outcome. We invited staff to share their own stories about when they had felt included in the workplace. Rather than creating yet another training video, we would take those real stories and turn them into an entertaining film that would demonstrate the benefit of diversity and inclusion. And so the Real Stories Project was brought to life.

The outcome of the campaign was a short film called *Work Mate* that was inspired by the real story of an employee with a vision impairment who regularly competed in triathlons, had hiked up Africa's tallest peak and run the Kokoda trail—with zero vision! In our story, Bruce, an able-bodied employee, tries to avoid his new desk buddy, Hamish, because he had never met a person with a vision impairment and felt too awkward around him. Bruce eventually has to lower his barriers when he is tricked into going on a tandem bike ride with Hamish just to prove he is not afraid of people with disability. The only problem was that Bruce had never learnt how to ride a bike. The pair had to learn how to work together to overcome their hurdles.

The film was extremely successful. A post-campaign survey showed that 97% of staff had engaged in discussion about inclusion and there had been an 80% increase in confidence in employing a person with disability. The film had also picked up a lovely collection of awards from film festivals around the world. The project had kept us extremely busy and had been a lot of hard work, but we were thrilled with the results.

To help retain a healthy life balance amongst a lot of busyness, we had adopted a simple yet powerful mentality from Dr Stephen Covey called The Big Rocks Theory. The idea is if you had to fit a pile of rocks, pebbles and sand into a jar, it is best to start with the largest rocks and work down in size to the sand. The pebbles will fit in around the rocks, and then likewise the sand.

If you start with the pebbles or the sand, there won't be enough room in the jar for the larger rocks to fit. This illustration of priorities had opened my eyes.

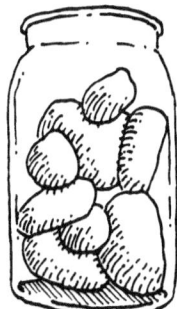 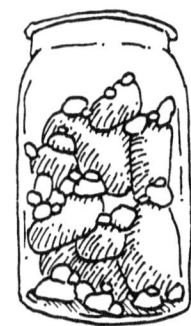 

In the past, I had tried for many years to book in little breaks when work would allow. But this only meant that we never got a break because there was always something going on at work. So the following year on January 1st, I sat down and opened up a fresh new calendar for the year. I went through every month and booked in all of the events that we considered to be our big rocks: a weekend away for Genevieve's birthday, my birthday, trips to visit our families, a two-week holiday mid-way through the year, a couple of long weekends off with friends, a Christmas break. We didn't yet know the details of our plans, but the dates were blacked out and we would work out the details later.

The technique worked sensationally well. My team all has access to each other's work calendars and when they saw that I was booked to be away, they just scheduled meetings and work project schedules around my availabilities. The pebbles and sand were dropping in nicely around the big rocks.

I was grateful we had implemented this new system when we were invited back to run Australia Post's Real Stories Project campaign again, this time creating a bigger project. For the returning year, we created a six-part comedy series that had, once again, been inspired by the real-life stories of Australia Post staff. The series was extremely successful (more details of this to come) and Australia Post were absolutely thrilled. But the success had come at a personal cost.

We had pushed ourselves to our absolute limits to pull off the comedy series. Because we were so passionate about the potential of the project, we had been overly optimistic about how much we could achieve within the limited budget we had been given. With only a small crew and a week to shoot thirty minutes of content, we had pushed ourselves with long fifteen-plus-hour days. We'd had a young and eager filmmaker from Adelaide come and volunteer as a production assistant but because the budget was so tight, we couldn't afford to offer her accommodation so she stayed on a blow-up mattress at our house for a week. Each night, the three of us would arrive back home late, collapse into our beds, then wake up early the next morning to get back onto set. By the end of the week we were completely burnt out.

At the same time Genevieve was spending a lot of time putting out fires at Bus Stop Films. They had partnered with an organisation to fund and produce an inclusive short film but midway through production it was clear this organisation was not a good fit as a partner. They were overly demanding, did not come through with what they had agreed to and it was clear that they were just keen to piggyback on the success of Bus Stop. It was becoming Genevieve's crash course in conflict resolution and she was now absolutely exhausted from trying to resolve a relentless battle.

We were both desperate for a break. We had been running non-stop for months and were about to fall in a heap. The light at the end of the tunnel was that we had our annual holiday booked just around the corner. This year we had lined up a getaway to New Zealand to coincide with the completion of our project for Australia Post. We had been to New Zealand before and discovered a couple of quiet sanctuaries that we knew we could return to for some overdue rest and rejuvenation. One particular spot is a sleepy town called Akaroa just over an hour's drive out of Christchurch on the South Island. A little town with a rich French history nestled in the remnants of an old volcano, the area is known for its colonies of seals, penguins and frequent visits from the dolphins. It was a perfect spot for some much needed recovery.

Unfortunately, once we had settled into our beautiful little B&B, the phone calls for Genevieve didn't stop. And when they did subside for a moment, she was overcome with anxiety. One evening, the calls continued from dinner all the way through to 3 am. By this point we were both well and truly exhausted and feeling very stressed. The fact that this was our only holiday for the year and we both desperately needed to unwind weighed heavily on our minds.

A few days into our trip, we journeyed north to a homestay I had randomly found on Airbnb. Online it looked like a quaint hobby farm, but what I didn't know was that the property was tucked so far up into a valley that there was no phone reception or WI-FI. It was completely off the grid and the nearest point for reception was an hour's drive back towards the previous town.

As we approached the property we were met with a white-washed stone cottage surrounded by garden beds overflowing with flowers, fruit trees and vegetables. We pulled into the driveway and a proud peacock fanned its vibrant tail feathers, the pet pig trotted out to greet us and a three-day-old goat bounced out after the owner as she came out of the house to welcome us to her home.

We had no choice but to completely disconnect from the world. We were terrified of what might happen while we were offline. But it turned out to be the exact thing that we needed. Instead of stressing about work, we went for long walks along the river. Instead of taking calls from difficult businesses, we ate freshly caught lobster on the front balcony. Rather than respond to a flurry of emails, we sat up late by a bonfire and toasted marshmallows. After a couple of days, our minds began to unwind, our heart rates slowed back down and we started to feel like our old selves again.

Sadly, four days later when we continued on our journey through the South Island, our phones pinged back to life as we drove back into reception's range and we were bombarded again with issues back at work. I wish I could say that we had learnt from this trip to protect our down-time, but this pattern continued year after year.

Five years later, I purchased a second phone just for work, and removed email, calendar notifications and all of the work-related apps from my personal phone. The plan was to leave the work phone back with my operations director whenever we took time off so could try to switch off. Surely now on our annual holiday, this time up to sunny Byron Bay, with auto-responders all activated and my work phone 765 kilometres away, we could disconnect from work? Could Genevieve and I unwind and focus just on each other? Alas, work still found us.

While I was sitting by the pool and reading my book, some of my team assessed a situation and deemed it necessary to call my personal phone to keep me informed. Off the back of one of my senior staff members submitting their resignation just a week prior, another senior member had been offered a role elsewhere that better suited his skill sets and he was going to finish up at Taste. He was happy to stay on for two months to finish out his role well, but had thought it imperative that I know this information immediately, not five days later when I was due to return back to the office. I've come to peace with the fact that staff members come and go. It used to really upset me when someone would leave, as we had invested so much time personally into each person, but I've learnt that some people stay for long seasons and some for short. Either way, it's not forever. But this one time, it felt more difficult as I had two senior roles move on within a week. As much as I tried to put it out of my mind, I fell into an anxious slump and the rest of our vacation was a write-off.

My conclusion is that perhaps it is an unrealistic expectation for leaders and entrepreneurs to be able to completely switch off an entire part of their lives. Even with countermeasures in place, things are bound to slip through. Rather than fight it, Genevieve and I have finally found a better solution. We are now more prepared for little disruptive things creeping into our holidays. We still do what we can to divert these things before a break, but when they do arise, we have become better at dealing with them swiftly. We acknowledge to each other that something has come up, we switch back into 'work mode' to deal with it as quickly as possible, then close that door and switch back off. From too many ruined holidays, we understand the damage done by not dealing with these issues in the moment and instead carrying it around with us for the duration of our downtime.

Wouldn't you rather be sitting back, eating fresh lobster and looking out over the New Zealand countryside? I know I would.

TAKEAWAYS

Healthy life balance comes from good organisation. Prioritise booking in the important events first and then schedule the other work activities around them.

It's unrealistic to expect to be able to completely switch off. Prepare for the little disruptions with a plan in place.

PART FOUR

Purpose at Work

CHAPTER FOURTEEN | **MOUNTAINS AND VALLEYS**

This Was the Hardest Decision I Ever Had to Make

As we found our groove working with large corporations to create their video content, we quickly discovered the true meaning of feast or famine. Based on the peaks of the workloads, we saw a strong pipeline of work and had grown our team of eight up to eleven to match the demand. But, because we worked from project to project, we would swing between weeks of more work than we could handle and then weeks with not enough work to keep our team busy. When we were busy, life was great: plenty of revenue coming in, happy clients and a team that was motivated, focussed and producing fantastic creative content. But in the famous words of Mike Tyson, 'Everyone has a plan until they get punched in the mouth.'

We had launched into the new year with a very strong outlook. A full pipeline and a list of work orders were going to keep our team very busy for the next six months. Then, in the space of a week, we got calls from a couple of clients letting us know they would need to delay, re-scope or cancel their projects. This wasn't unusual as there is always change in demand, but these happened to be our biggest three projects in our pipeline. We were resourced for a very busy start to the year, but would now have next to nothing to put our team on. It was clear that we were about to start haemorrhaging cash if we didn't do something. And whatever we were to do, we needed to do it quickly.

After an emergency board meeting one Saturday night, we determined that we would need to lay off a third of our team and downsize our premises. Initially, I wasn't too concerned about our office; it was our team that I was most worried about. We had put so much time into building a strong culture that we had all grown very close and our colleagues felt like family.

The next evening, Genevieve and I drove to each of the homes of our colleagues who we would be letting go.

We sat together and shared the difficult news that we would have to say goodbye. Making the time to sit with each staff member made all the difference. There were, of course, tears, but I was amazed at how understanding they all were. I think they understood better than I did that at the end of the day it was a job, not a family.

Next was to downsize our office. Our beautiful studio was definitely too big for us. It certainly looked the part of a high-flying production company, but looks weren't paying the bills. Over the years we had discovered the pulse of our business and realised that we didn't need such a large space. We had envisioned that our clients would want to come out to us for regular meetings, creative workshops and project reviews, but we were too far from public transport and car parking was difficult so, in the end, it was more convenient for us to go to them. We had built a soundproof edit suite but our editors had preferred to work out in the communal area with the rest of the team. And then, of course, we had set up lots of desks and work spaces for our team and freelancers but they were regularly out filming on location or at meetings so often the studio would only have one or two people in it.

Even with all this, I found letting go of the office was personally more difficult than I had expected. I realised I had connected an unhealthy amount of my own identity and personal worth into that space. Over the years, I had led the charge with our renovations; the fit-out and decor of the studio had become an extension of who I was. I had been very proud to be able to show people around our space and have the means to host events for our community, from an engagement party for one of our colleagues to industry nights, film premieres and *World of Warcraft* LAN parties* with staff.

So it was sad to say goodbye to our studio, but my revelation that a part of my identity had been in a building was a healthy eye-opener. I vowed not to invest so much of my identity into our studio or our work.

We packed up our things and moved to an office in the city that was a quarter of the size and very close to public transport. It was in a building with about fifty other companies that shared amenities, comfortable lounge room spaces and private

---

* LAN parties = local area network parties where a whole bunch of people cram into the studio, BYO computer and we all join the same network to play multiplayer games against each other late into the night, often accompanied by bouts of singing, loud jeering and plenty of good food.

meeting rooms. This model was a much better fit as it would allow us to expand and contract the size of our team as needed. I knew we were facing a difficult new season and it was going to take a lot of energy and focus. We had to win a number of large projects and put in some long hours to ensure they were as profitable as possible.

There are seasons when we are at the top of the mountain—you can see clearly ahead, you're kicking goals and life is great. Then there are seasons when we have to walk through the valley—it is dark, each day can feel like a trudge, it's hard work and you can lose sight of where you are going. I knew we were going down into a valley.

This is part of the deal if you're ambitious and want to get to the top of mountains: there are always going to be valleys to journey through. When you get to the summit of one mountain, it is exciting and relieving. But, of course, we don't then stop forever at the top of a mountain. We go on. And so you set your sights on the next mountain, but to get there you have to go down into another valley. Valleys can be tiring, difficult, lonely and feel unrewarding, but there is no way to get to the top of the next mountain without going through them.

As our aspirations get bigger and the peaks of the mountains rise in height, so too do the depth of the valleys. The challenges get bigger, but while the journey through the valleys may also become harder, the base of each subsequent valley is rarely as low as the previous one. Big challenges become less scary because we've been through challenges before, and we know we will come back out the other side. We are always rising, even when we go into a valley, if that makes sense.

A major challenge in our twenty-first-century Western world is that we seldom publicly share the moments from our valleys, and certainly not while we are travelling through one. When our society is only promoting the personal and professional highlights reel, it is easy to presume that no one else is going through a difficult time. It seems that everyone is on a constant streak of project wins, new staff hires, holidays in exotic places and groups of friends, arm-in-arm with big smiles on their faces. But all great leaders are constantly going in and out of valleys. The journey towards a goal is not a continuous ascent; there are plenty of ups and downs.

When I was a kid, my dad would take me out bushwalking with him. He is an avid bushwalker* and delights in the challenge of navigating long walks through unknown terrain all over the world. A successful bushwalk is all about the preparation. We would load up our backpacks with supplies for numerous days: a tent, warm clothes, food, sleeping bags and plenty of water. But my favourite thing to pack was the scroggin**.

---

* And still is today. As he approaches seventy, his challenge is not his health, but convincing his friends to keep coming.
** Or as it's more commonly known: trail mix. But don't you think 'scroggin' has such a great sound to it? I'll stick with that.

A bag of scroggin contains a mix of nuts, dried fruit and a smattering of lollies or chocolates. You'd carry in your pocket, or even better, in a bumbag at the front for easy access while walking. A couple of mouthfuls would be just the boost you needed when your energy started to fade on a walk*.

Out on a bush walk or not, scroggin is still just as important in my life today. Scroggin is the boost we intentionally take with us into the valleys to help us get through. While it looks a bit different today to a pouch of fruit and nuts, I have found having a little bag of tricks at the ready has hugely helped to endure some of the longer and more challenging valleys. Taking my dog for a walk, early morning gym sessions, keeping a gratitude journal, cooking a favourite meal for the family, organising a date night with Genevieve. These things usually drop in importance during a hard time, but they are so often just the booster I need to get through and so making the time to do them regularly is a game changer.

---

* I have to confess, I haven't been out on a long bushwalk with my dad for nearly two decades. Most likely because on our last trip together it rained non-stop for the last two days and we had no choice but to walk in soggy clothes from sunrise to sunset. Getting into a damp sleeping bag at the end of a long day's walk wasn't my idea of a good time.

Journeying through valleys is not only good for us, it also helps us to be real with others. The wonderful Brené Brown teaches on the beauty that comes from the darkness in the valleys. Only once we ourselves have gone through the darkness can we be truly present with another person in their darkness. As a fixer by nature, I used to find it very difficult to just sit and be with people when they were going through a difficult season. I would want to get in there to offer advice, find a solution and encourage them to keep going. And, certainly, sometimes this sort of blind, faith-filled encouragement can be helpful. But there have been many times that I've just needed to sit quietly with someone in a challenging time and reassure them that I genuinely understood. Often they just needed to know that there was someone with them who could listen and understand.

So, as we downsized our team and moved to a smaller office, our awareness that we were heading down into a valley this season made it that much easier to stay energised and focussed. I sat the team down and laid out the plans for how we were going to navigate through the valley to successfully climb out the other side and up to the top of our next mountain. I painted the picture that we had been trying to manoeuvre a big and slow cruise ship, but now we were downsizing, shifting our priorities and reshaping ourselves to operate like a much smaller, faster and more nimble yacht. With this direction, our team was motivated and energised to take on what lay ahead.

And would you believe it, just six months later we had turned the business around. We had restructured the team, everyone had taken on more responsibilities and we were producing some of the best work we had ever created. As the end of the year approached, I took our team out for a celebratory Christmas dinner at Sydney's iconic Circular Quay. I had told the team to meet down at the harbour and we'd head out for a nice dinner. But instead of going to a restaurant, I led them down to a jetty where a private yacht awaited us for our evening on the water. We had come out of the valley and our business and team were more nimble and stronger than we had ever been before.

TAKEAWAYS

Empathy and respect makes all the difference. Building a strong culture does not prevent the need for layoffs, but showing empathy and respect in the process makes a big difference.

Difficult times are a natural part of success. There is no way to get to the top of the next mountain without going through a valley.
But challenges become less scary with the knowledge that we have journeyed through this before.

Be prepared for the valleys. Having a little bag of tricks at the ready helps to sustain through the longer and more challenging seasons.

Enduring difficult times helps us to be real with others. Only once we have gone through the darkness can we be truly present with another person in their darkness.

CHAPTER FIFTEEN | HONOURING FAILURE

Everyone Deserves the Right to Fail

At both Taste and Bus Stop Films, we have very strong foundations in equal access. Everyone deserves the opportunity to participate and succeed in life. When Genevieve first met Gerard passionately reciting Shakespeare in his doorway, here stood a young man with immense talent who had never been given the opportunity to succeed with his acting. For years, he had been seeking an opportunity, but people saw his disability first and discounted his potential. And most likely, from the kindness of their hearts, they surmised that he had a high chance of failing and so wanted to protect him from that dejection. But here lies the problem ... everyone deserves not just the opportunity to succeed, but also the opportunity to fail.

It is in our failings that we have the opportunity to learn and grow the most.

Shortly after I met Genevieve and had started attending her church, Kirrily, one of the church leaders, heard that I was a creative type and had done a bit of design and animation. She had had a dream about creating a series of children's books to teach kids about life values and virtues in an easy-to-understand way. What I liked about Kirrily's writing was that she didn't want to make Christian books for Christian kids. She wanted to connect with all kids. So when she took a look at some of my work and asked if I would be interested in illustrating her first book, I was pretty excited by the opportunity.

By this point I already had my mantra of 'say yes and figure it out later' firmly in place, so I committed to the project and then set to work figuring out how to create a kids' book. I was a passionate drawer and had studied art through high school and my short-lived university degree, but never illustrated an actual book like this. So I drew on what I knew: the types of craft activities Mum had done with us when we were kids. She was an art teacher so we never had paint-by-number or store-bought craft activity sets. Instead, she taught us to rely on our imaginations and create fantastical things with objects around the house: cardboard boxes, old wrapping paper, empty tissue boxes, toilet paper rolls; whatever we could get our hands on. As a five-year-old, my most prized possession was a hot glue gun I had been gifted for my birthday with a big pack of popsicle sticks.

I wanted to pass on this gift of using your imagination to other kids to inspire them to get out and play. So I set about crafting imagery for the first book by scanning high resolution images of textures I could easily find like envelopes, old magazines, corrugated cardboard, birthday cards, handmade papers and pages from old novels. I drew the characters and scenery for each page by hand and then digitally recreated each layout by cutting out pieces of the textured scans for each piece of the image. The result was a wonderful collage created from everyday household objects. Thankfully, Kirrily was thrilled because the process had taken weeks to create and I wasn't too keen on starting again.

That's when Kirrily broke the news that this was only Book One in a series of nine books that she wanted to create. Unfortunately for me, I hadn't heard of any children's book illustrators who had retired early on their yacht, so I decided not to quit my day job and illustrating Kirrily's books became a passion project on the side. And because each book took so long to illustrate, we set our goal on releasing one book each year*.

As an artist herself, my mum loved seeing each book come to life and observing a bit of her influence in my illustration style. One summer she had gone through some difficult health challenges and I had planned to nip back to the Adelaide Hills for a weekend to see how she was doing. As a surprise, I had held onto an advanced copy of the next book in the series and decided to gift her with it, hopefully to lift her spirits a little. Once I arrived back in my old home, we sat down at the kitchen table and I watched expectantly as she opened the book and flicked through the pages.

From time to time she would look up with a smile, recognising little details or influences from my childhood in the artwork. But when she got to one page her expression changed from interest, to intrigue, to mild confusion.

---

* Well, roughly a book a year ... ten years on and we've only just released book seven of the nine-part series!

She tilted her head, squinted her eyes and then looked at me with a concerned expression. 'Did you get someone to proofread this before printing?' We most certainly had. By this stage, we didn't have a publisher so Kirrily and her husband, Tim, had personally covered the costs of the print run. So we had, indeed, asked multiple people to scrutinise each page before it had gone to print.

She checked across the illustration again and pointed out what had caught her attention. I leant in to see what she had seen and my heart plummeted straight down into my gut; I had indeed made a huge mistake. In the rush to finish the book on time, I had cut a corner and downloaded a texture from the internet rather than scanning in my own as I usually did. At first glance, the texture was exactly what I needed: a page of small printed writing from an old novel which I would cut up into long, thin strips, rendering the actual text itself irrelevant as surely no one would take the time to try and read the random smattering of words. But Mum did.

Of all the books this page could have been from, it turned out to be from an old erotic novel. Short excerpts of titillating text could just be made out in the picture of this newly printed children's book. 'His member throbbed ...' 'She groaned as he ...' 'He caressed her bare ...'

Needless to say, I was mortified. Not so much for having been exposed for cutting a corner, but the fact that Kirrily had just printed two thousand copies of these books and they had already been shipped out to distributors across the country. And also my plan to surprise Mum with something nice had failed spectacularly. But my biggest challenge was yet to come: I had to break the news to Kirrily and Tim.

They are both exceptionally lovely people. I expected Kirrily to be shocked and then forgiving, but Tim is a no-nonsense businessman and surely this sort of expensive mistake would have consequences. And physically, he's a big unit so I was terrified.

I stepped outside onto the balcony of my childhood home and dialled Kirrily's number. Her ever-bright and cheery voice answering the call didn't help. At my request she called in her husband, Tim, put me on speaker phone and I nervously dropped my news.

Their reaction to my panic was a masterclass in understanding and forgiveness. They didn't fly off the handle, they didn't yell or unfurl a list of consequences. While shocked and certainly very concerned, they immediately knew from my own mortified tone that it was a genuine mistake. I was so relieved but immediately taken by surprise by their very next question: 'Was I ok?' Even after dropping this problem on their doorstep, I was their first concern.

Kirrily immediately recalled the latest release and set about reissuing hundreds of copies of the book, this time without the adult erotica. As I went back inside after my call, I passed Dad in the corridor. 'You'll laugh at this one day,' he said with a sheepish grin on his face. 'But probably not for quite a while.'*

Back in Sydney, barely six months later, one of our designers came to me with a look of panic on her face that I recognised immediately. For weeks she had been working on a large print campaign for one of our biggest clients and she'd just received the designs back from the printers only to find a typo

---

* Dad tells me he has kept one of the original copies and has it tucked away in a hiding place he refuses to divulge. He attests it's in the hope that one day he can sell it and make his fortune.

on the front page. Thousands of copies had been printed and were on their way to the client. With Kirrily and Tim's response still very fresh in my mind, I had no hesitation to stand alongside our employee and help them to rectify the issues. It cost us thousands to reprint the job, but using the situation to ensure our staff felt safe at work was invaluable.

CEO of Disney, Bob Iger says: 'If you want innovation—and you should, always—you need to give permission to fail.' Staff, co-workers, freelancers, family, friends: they all need space to fail. If people live in a world where they are so fearful of making a mistake, they will only ever stay where it is safe and never step out to try something new. We have to give our people that safe space.

But what about for ourselves? Do you also allow room for your own failings?

In 2017, I was very fortunate to spend some time at the UsTwo studios in London. UsTwo had shot to fame three years prior with the release of their independent IOS game *Monument Valley*. Heavily inspired by the gravity-defying staircases and architectural drawings of M. C. Escher, I had fallen in love with the artistry of the game as soon as it was released.

UsTwo co-founder Mils, was kind enough to not only make time to meet with Genevieve and I at their Shoreditch studios, but offered us a creative home to work from while we were in town. Spread out over three brightly painted levels, the firm's headquarters welcomed people in and fostered creativity and innovation. Mils shared the journey of the game and how, just like nearly every success story, *Monument Valley* was the culmination of many failed launches.

I returned to Australia inspired and re-energised for a similar project of our own. As with the origins of *Monument Valley*, we had been working away on a story-based product in our downtime. A year prior, Genevieve had written a beautiful short script titled 'I Didn't Like Hubert 'about a loud and colourful boy who didn't fit into the dull and greyscale world he lived in. With our growing production team and our expanding skill set in digital production, I had been excited to flex our muscles and turn this into an interactive animated ebook.

From the outset, it seemed relatively straightforward but it would end up taking us two and a half years to create and it pushed us to our technical limits. We had produced so many beautiful animations before, but to do so for a digital platform, one where the user could control the characters and timings, was incredibly difficult.

The end result was stunning. Each fantastical scene had been beautifully designed by Alex, our Art Director; Javed had designed our two main characters; our design team had conjured up a spectacular cast of leaf trolls, dragons, flying rhinoceros and clockwork mice; our composer had scored a suite of gorgeous music; and Jared, our web developer, had spent weeks writing code to bring all of the characters to life at the control of the viewer. I had flown to Los Angeles to record the voice-overs with a celebrity as the narrator.

We launched the project as an animated ebook on the App Store and had committed to donating 100% of the profit to the Humpty Dumpty Foundation with the goal of raising $30,000 to purchase lifesaving equipment for premature babies. We organised a launch event, recruited a PR agency to help us secure publicity and interviews on TV and promoted the project to every single contact in our database. I was confident it was going to be a huge success.

It absolutely bombed.

Failed spectacularly.

A complete nose-dive.

Reaching nowhere near our initial target of raising $30,000, it raised a measly $300. We hit just 1% of our goal. And then, after a week or two of declining rating numbers, it disappeared into App Store obscurity completely. I was dumbfounded. It had been years of hard work, passion and love, giving it everything we had.

But all the way through, there had been one teeny weeny problem: I had been striving, not striding. A small alphabetical difference, but a big attitudinal distinction.

Striving is to have your eyes completely locked on a goal in the future which you are pursuing at any cost. This is how I had been operating on this project for the past months.

Whereas to _stride_ is to have a clear picture of the future goal but be able to move towards it harmoniously within your and your team's capabilities. One approach is healthy and balanced; the other is a manic work ethic that ensures you won't be happy until you reach the goal. If you even reach the goal.

The end of _Hubert's_ story is not that I learnt a lesson and then later had a roaring success. The ebook completely failed. But the lessons from this experience have become invaluable in how I work and lead. When you watch young children play together in a sandpit, they don't need to be taught how to build a sandcastle. They learn through instinct and trial and error. Try one thing, it doesn't work, you try another. The Dean of Pixar University, Randy Nelson, says, 'You have to honour failure, because failure is just the negative space around success.'

Before Randy, Japanese potters discovered this beauty in failure centuries ago. 'Kintsugi', which translates to 'golden joinery', originated in the late fifteenth century when potters would repair a broken pot or vase with a special lacquer dusted with powdered gold or silver. What many would see as a failed pot would become a highly valued and unique work of art with the glimmers of gold shining through the cracks. I like to think we humans are like these pots.

While the pain from *Hubert's* failure was very real and my confidence took a knock, I am so grateful to have had the opportunity to fail, pick myself back up, and go again. The successes I have enjoyed since then are largely due to the learnings from my numerous trials and errors.

TAKEAWAYS

Everyone deserves the opportunity to fail. The experiences to fail is just as important as the opportunity to succeed as it allows for learning, innovation and growth.

To thrive is to stride, not strive. Set a clear picture of the future goal with the ability to move towards it harmoniously without sacrificing balance in life.

CHAPTER SIXTEEN | **MANIPULATION VS MOTIVATION**

How We Increased Viewership by 14,000%

When I was a child, I saw a frizzy-haired magician by the name of Raymond Crowe perform at a local talent show and I was absolutely captivated. Dressed smartly in a tuxedo but moving with a Charlie Chaplin-like gait, he marched out onto the stage carrying nothing more than a violin case. From the variety of performances that had just preceded him, I was preparing to hear a classical performance from this awkward violinist. But as he reached the centre of the stage, he almost toppled over. His violin case had become completely stuck in mid-air.

As if by magic, the case had frozen in time and left its carrier to figure out the consequences. The magician pulled and pulled at the handle, then he walked all the way around it and tried to push it with all his might but the case appeared to be firmly stuck in mid-air. Finally, after much trying, he called for his assistant, his young son with hair as frizzy as his dad's, who marched out onto stage, clearly unimpressed to be called upon. The young apprentice simply gave the case a flick with his finger and it fell to the ground. The illusion was complete and I was hooked. I absorbed the rest of his act from the edge of my seat: dozens of cards appearing from nowhere, inconceivable shadow puppetry set to Louis Armstrong music, and a coat jacket coming to life and dancing across the stage.

The very next week, I joined the Australian Society of Magicians* to begin a journey to learn the art of misdirection, distraction and deceit, all in the name of entertainment. I loved illusions in the simple and everyday objects. Disappearing and reappearing cans of Coke, newspapers tearing in half and then re-forming, nails passing right through balloons without making them burst. As magicians in training, we would manipulate our audiences to think one thing while we did another, ultimately to get the behavioural response we were looking for—awe, wonder and surprise. Magic was all about manipulation.

---

* Well, the youth division to be precise. And yes, of course we had a cool name: The Young Adelaide Magicians Society, or YAMS for short. If that wasn't going to impress the ladies, I don't know what would.

For profit-led organisations and leaders, manipulation is a key tool in the kit. To yield the results they are after, they need to ensure the consumer does as they need them to do. The difference between magicians and leaders is that everyone is expecting the magician to manipulate them.

Take fast food. We know that most fast food is not good for us. Yet every day, why do millions of people make this their meal of choice? As consumers, we are pushed to eat a greasy fast food burger, and made to feel as if it was our own choice. Taste, convenience, visual appeal. The fast food business knows it's not good for you, yet they are very happy to take your money in exchange for you receiving very few nutritional benefits and ongoing health complications. Their will over yours.

That is why there is a multi-billion dollar industry that serves to make cognitive dissonance work: advertising. Advertising exists to change or reinforce (manipulate) behaviour in favour of a product or service. Much of what we experience through advertising which causes that behavioural change is informed by cognitive dissonance: thoughts influence feelings, which in turn influence actions, the sum of which equals behaviour. We experience something and it makes us feel a certain way, affirming or challenging. If affirming, we continue down that path, confirmed by what we've seen. If, however, our own thoughts/feelings/beliefs/prior notions are challenged enough, we will do something to change the situation, thus changing our behaviour.

THOUGHTS —INFLUENCE→ FEELINGS ←INFLUENCE— ACTIONS = BEHAVIOURAL CHANGE

Advertising tactics range from the simple to the complex. A simple behavioural change could be 'reframing' a more expensive product to be more noticeable, thus increasing the chance of an individual choosing that item. For example, reframing more expensive items in a café as more tempting options, placing them higher in the menu, is a useful way to steer customers to choose those items over a cheaper option.

Another mechanism is to use 'collectivism' to coerce behaviour based on what other people are doing because, at the end of the day, a very strong human driver is acceptance. Deep down we all want to fit in and belong, to some degree. When you take kids to the annual agricultural show, they will inevitably want to eat whatever they see other kids walking around eating, so adults will often find themselves traipsing around the food truck aisles trying to find that same toffee apple/milkshake/corn on the cob to appease a screaming child. Even well-meaning charities will use this technique to get the behaviour they desire with campaigns like Pink Ribbon Day, Daffodil Day or Red Nose Day that encourage you to fit in with everyone else.

For a more overtly manipulative industry, look no further than gambling. Take poker machines. The pokies is an incredibly tough behavioural change brief: make people want to give their money to something that, in exchange, will give them one in a 9.7 million chance of getting exponential value in return*. Coercing people to walk through the door of an establishment with pokies would be a very hard task without any form of manipulation.

Instead, using a common marketing technique called 'eliminating complexity', gambling companies can manipulate users for hours. Once in the door and seated at a machine, the behaviour they want is for people to drop money into their machines for as long as possible, to increase the amount of profit

---

* You can check out more of these terrifying stats at the Australian Gambling Help Online website: www.gamblinghelponline.org.au/understanding-gambling/what-are-the-odds

they can make, of course. By eliminating as many complexities for the user as possible, this becomes more and more achievable. Design of the interface is constantly stimulating, button size is increased so it is dead-easy to find and press, there is minimal amount of time between rounds to retain engagement, and regularly timed sounds of apparent wins, off in the distance, are manufactured to remind the consumer of the chance of winning. It extends to even perfecting the angle of the screen to minimise fatigue and removing any indicators of real-world time such as windows to the outside world or clocks, ensuring customers can easily lose track of time. Despite there being a higher chance of being struck by lightning than hitting the jackpot, users are manipulated to believe they'll get the value they are seeking.

So what's an alternative to manipulation? The other side of the coin is motivation. People are not pushed to do something; instead they are independently motivated to want to change their own behaviour. Motivation is found in a truth that people can connect to. And when it is grounded within a purpose-led foundation to solve a problem not primarily driven by profit, for an individual/community/environment, people are far more likely to want to get onboard and will deliberately alter their behaviour to align themselves.

We discovered this when we were creating the Australia Post series, The Real Stories Project. With a top-down approach, Post was already hiring and including a diverse workforce but the staff were mostly unaware of the benefits. So our brief had been to create a campaign that would increase staff confidence to employ a person with a disability. The task was simple enough, but engagement and retention would be difficult. How could we attract and retain the attention of forty thousand postal staff spread out across the country, with the majority of these staff not sitting in front of a computer, but spending most of their time out on postie bikes delivering the country's mail?

As staff were not forced to watch the proposed film, our solution was to tell an authentic and highly relatable story—one of their own. The intention was to engage and entertain for we knew that from the get-go we did not have a captive audience. We needed to earn the attention of our audience.

We put out an invitation for all of the staff to share a moment when they had felt included in the workplace. What had happened, why had they been included, how did it make them feel? Post staff were intrigued and stories began to trickle in. Over the coming weeks, our inbox began to fill up with amazing stories of kindness, hope and some of the best traits of humanity on show. With a winning story in hand, we were able to create the short film *Work Mate* with the deliberate intention of capturing and retaining the attention of our postal audience rather than primarily delivering a corporate message. We surmised that if the film was engaging enough, staff would hopefully be motivated to tell their colleagues and family members about it, and would even want to watch it at home after work.

The project did exactly that. As filmmakers, we had treated the brief not as a training video but as entertainment that happens to also educate and raise awareness of a corporate agenda. Staff were motivated to change. The internal metrics were great and word of the film had spread throughout the organisation.

When we were invited back the following year to run the call-out for stories again, we saw even greater results. Staff had loved getting involved in the storytelling process and being entertained with a film rather than being schooled through a dull corporate video. The second year, we had so many story submissions from staff that instead of one film, we were able to create a six-part comedy series about a local talent show and the diversity of skills that made it a success. This, too, was an immediate hit. Uptake was extremely high and staff were becoming more and more confident to employ and work with people who were different to them.

Our theory that people would make a behavioural change and even share the content with others if authentically motivated to do so was 100% accurate. This follow-up campaign would go on to exceed even our highest expectations when the national broadcaster, the Australian Broadcasting Corporation, requested the TV broadcast rights, and Qantas airlines acquired the films to run on their inflight entertainment on every domestic flight in Australia. Overnight, the potential viewership of the films leapt from 33,000 postal workers to 4.2 million people across the country. Manipulation was nowhere to be found. This was purely the power of motivation at its finest.

TAKEAWAYS

Behavioural change starts with a persons thoughts. And there are two key ways to influence thought; manipulation or motivation.

Motivation derives from a relatable truth. It empowers people to independently want to change a behaviour because it is best for them and because they genuinely want to.

CHAPTER SEVENTEEN | STORYTELLING
Great Leaders Are Storytellers

Beginning with prehistoric cave paintings then medieval ballads sung in castle halls, to nursery rhymes chanted in playgrounds to today's one billion monthly viewers on Tik Tok*, people have always used stories to communicate, teach and entertain each other. But so much more powerful than that, stories deeply connect us to each other or, as Eugene H. Peterson puts it, 'Stories are verbal acts of hospitality.'

From birth, we are taught to love stories. My twin girls have only just turned one and they can be in the middle of a screaming

---

* As of the start of 2023. As you read this it's likely either way more, or everyone's already moved onto the next big thing. You can check out the fascinating stats for yourself: www.demandsage.com/tiktok-user-statistics

fit, but when we pull out a storybook and start reading, they immediately calm down and are captivated. But a love of stories is not just limited to children. As adults, we love hearing stories. Similarly, storytelling should not just be limited to filmmakers, poets, novelists and songwriters. Storytelling is for everyone, and for leaders, storytelling is the most powerful tool in the belt.

And it is powerful because telling stories creates an emotional connection. As a mindset coach to many of Australia's top athletes and business leaders around the world, Ben Crowe loves storytelling. 'It is an irrational emotional connection that causes us to love the things we love,' Crowe teaches in his leadership coaching, 'and the way to get that emotional connection the best is storytelling.'

Casting a vision and telling the story of where we are going opens a door for people to be able to willingly come on the ride of their own accord, rather than being dragged along against their will. It allows for buy-in and showing others where we are going, before we arrive at our destination.

When we had to downsize and relocate our offices in 2017, I painted a picture of how our new space could work—how we would now be spending more time out on projects rather than in an office, how close we would be to public transport and the bounty of interesting new lunch places that would now surround us. Though the new office we had found was in a cool, creative part of town, the space itself was uninspiring and small but as soon as we started moving in, the team had already caught the vision. They could see what I could see and we were excited to set out on this new adventure together.

As a leader, the ability to share a story is one of the best ways to motivate, connect with, engage and inspire a team. But what makes for a great story? Here's a couple of storytelling starting points …

When I created *Larry* as a teenager, I wasn't aware that I was being vulnerable by sharing a part of my story about being bullied as a kid. I probably didn't know much about the word 'vulnerability' back then. Being bullied was just something that I had experienced and I wanted to share the experience with others. What I understand now as a filmmaker is the incredible power of vulnerability when we share our stories. Vulnerability allows people in, it lowers the drawbridge and can create a degree of trust. It says to the audience, 'I trust you with my story' and, in return, when we hear a story with vulnerability we are transfixed and honoured to be entrusted with such an insight.

But vulnerability doesn't mean oversharing and exposing every detail of our lives for the benefit of a compelling story. The level of vulnerability must match the level of trust we have with an audience. And trust must be earnt. Presenting to a group of new acquaintances, I will often share a vulnerable story about myself to build a foundation of connection. But the level of vulnerability may only look like a semi-trivial detail of my personal life, such as an anecdote about my dog Greta dressed up in a rain jacket to avoid getting wet. I am not divulging highly private information, but I am offering a small part of my story to start to build a connection. Whereas presenting to a small group of trusted staff, I would likely open up about much deeper issues and share a personal insight or revelation to help bring a point I am making to life.

Secondly, structure is the good friend of a good story. Like in any good presentation, you would have heard the adage 'Tell them where you are going, go there, then tell them where you went.' This is a great and simple structure to empower your audience to know where the story is going, but it is just as important for the storyteller. No one wants to listen to a person talk aimlessly until they find their way to the point they are trying to make. As the guide to your audience, structuring your story pays respect to those who are willing to listen.

Next, the best stories feature a character with a transformational arc—a change of character, something they've discovered or a revelation. Audiences want to see change. If there's no change or no development, audiences quickly get bored and disengage. That's why I share my revelations, the story behind my change of mind or how something changed me as a person. This can really start to get into the vulnerability space, particularly when Instagram is awash with highlight reels, Linkedin is jam-packed with bragging announcements and Twitter is loaded with loud opinions from people who never think themselves wrong. Share how you have changed as a person and the audience is much more likely to give you their time.

Fourth, keep your story relatable. Everyday stories are powerful because they are relatable. We watch intergalactic superhero blockbusters and dreamy romantic comedies for escapism, but when we tell stories to each other, as in person to person, they don't need to be grand global tales of daring company takeovers or life-saving stories about when we saved a school bus of children*. The goal of a good story is fundamentally not to impress or outdo another, but to connect. When we open up and tell relatable stories, people on the receiving end open up as well and may even want to share a part of their story in return.

Sharing your story allows people in and empowers them to want to work with you. People like to work with people, as in _real_ people. Not perfect 'social media highlights' people, but people who know they are flawed (because we all are!), people who admit their mistakes and people who grow from their experiences.

Fifth little tip, use your words to paint a picture so others can see what you can see. This is particularly important when it comes to setting the vision for where you are going or the desired outcome of a project. Don't be afraid to use descriptive sentences to illustrate what you can see so that others can see it too. Take the time to articulate the little things that make your story, well, a story. Where did it take place, was it warm or cold, how did it make you feel, what could you smell?

---

* Full disclosure again, I haven't done either of these things. If I had heroically saved a school bus of children from some impending doom, I probably would have opened the chapter with this.

The detail might not feel relevant to the core story, but it helps to transport people there. As an audience, we like to get inspired and to use our imaginations. This also helps listeners to make an emotional connection.

Lastly, keep your story concise. This doesn't mean short; it just means keep it to the length it needs to be. No longer. I often get asked what's the best length of video for optimum user engagement: one minute, thirty seconds, seven seconds? My answer is always the same: the length doesn't matter as long as you're telling an interesting story. Point in case, in 2018 we made a twenty-minute short film called *Shakespeare in Tokyo*. Unbeknownst to us, our client, the Tokyo Metropolitan Government, ran the film as a YouTube pre-roll ad in the lead-up to the 2020 Tokyo Olympic Games. Videos in these ad spots are usually only five to ten seconds long and are all about quick, upfront attention-grabbing. Needless to say our film wasn't tailored for the YouTube pre-roll video slot. However, the film got hundreds of thousands of people watching in its entirety. The comments section is full of people sharing how they completely forgot about the video they had originally intended to watch and were instead captivated by our film. This is what a good story will do; people will sit and stay engaged for as long as the story is engaging.

TAKEAWAYS

Storytelling is foundational for everyone. Humans have always used stories to communicate, teach and entertain each other, and storytelling deeply connects us to each other.

Storytelling is one the most powerful tools in a leaders belt. Telling stories creates an emotional connection with people and allows for buy-in.

Vulnerability allows people in. It is a powerful tool for storytelling but the level of vulnerability should match the level of trust we have with the audience.

The best stories feature transformation. We always want to see a character with a transformational arc; learning something, growing as a person, solving the mystery or discovering something that they didn't know.

The goal of a good story is connection. When we open up and tell a relatable story, people will often open up in return.

CHAPTER EIGHTEEN | **CHARTING A COURSE**
Without a Destination I Nearly Ran Aground

It's not about the destination, it's about the journey. A great bumper sticker on the back of a retiree's caravan, but a difficult mantra for any leader.

The journey is important and there are usually a lot of lessons to be learnt on the way, but core to a leader's mission is to arrive at the destination. You wouldn't pay a plumber if they concluded a job and said, 'Sorry we didn't finish your new bathroom, but we did learn lots of lessons on the way.' We're programmed from an early age to set our focus on the destination and not give up until we get there. But the plans we make to get to our destinations often aren't the paths we mapped out at the beginning.

As a kid I loved sailing out on the river with my dad. We were fortunate to grow up with many summer holidays spent down at the mouth of the Murray River where Australia's longest river comes out to meet the ocean. My grandparents had built a holiday house for their kids when growing up, which we now all got to enjoy. By no means a five-star beach resort, 'The Shack', as it was lovingly known, was home to our childhood holidays spent fishing off the neighbour's jetty, canoeing through the long reeds, running short showers to preserve enough hot water to also wash the dishes, camping out under the stars with our cousins and having VHS movie nights because the TV reception wasn't quite strong enough for anything else. We adored it!

I loved being out on the water with Dad—the excitement of ducking under the boat's boom as it violently whipped from side to side in the wind, pulling up the centreboards and rudders so we wouldn't get bogged in the mud as we neared the river bank. I loved that Katie Forest, our rescue dog, would jump on board and insist that she come on every trip, but then leap off the boat at the end of every journey to swim the last hundred metres to the shore. Dad's boat wasn't fancy, just a small, orange fibreglass twin hull catamaran, but what it lacked in show, it made up for with fun.

With no motors, no batteries or steering wheel, sailing a boat relies on knowledge of how to catch the wind and navigate the current just right to help you to get to your destination. From the balcony of the shack, we could see dozens of these small sailboats whiz back and forth across the river all day long throughout the holidays. As a young child, my limited understanding of navigating a sailboat was that you were stuck sailing in the same direction until the wind changed, or if that didn't happen you might have to sail in the same direction the entire way around the globe to return to where you left off.

The day Dad deemed me ready to operate the boat myself was an exciting, coming-of-age day. In retrospect, it was probably just when my arms were long enough to reach the tiller (the long pole connected to the rudder). Regardless, it felt significant to me; I was put in charge of steering us to where we were going to go.

It turned out that steering and navigating were two very different things. When it comes to sailing, you can rarely just point and say, 'That's where I'm going' and then simply go there. You have to work with the conditions. I quickly found out that the key to success was twofold: determine the destination and then work with the conditions to get there.

Dad showed me first how to navigate to where I wanted to go by picking something on the horizon such as a brightly coloured beach house or a wonky shaped tree on the far side of the river. He would call this my 'tac': my destination marker and I had to remember to keep looking up and positioning the boat towards it. Then I could focus on working with the water current and weather conditions to help me get closer to our destination. Which way was the water moving, was it high tide or low tide, how fast was the wind blowing and from which direction?

The course to my destination was never a straight line; rather it was a messy zig-zag as I navigated the real-world conditions.

It wasn't until two decades later that I realised this is exactly what navigating as a leader looks like. First, we must determine the destination where we want to end up and then navigate through the ever changing conditions of life to help us get there. We can use the conditions that may appear as a deterrent, to help propel us forward. This path may result in a messy zig-zag, but if we keep looking up regularly to where we want to be heading, we can adjust the sails and get closer to our destination.

As a leader, one of the biggest traps I find is that if I don't set my sights on a destination at all, I will be dragged along by life's current. From the outside this often still looks like progress, as we're moving, but the problem is that the current is taking the crowd in the same direction. And for most leaders, this isn't the destination of choice. A pause for recalibration is better than momentum in the wrong direction.

One key difference I discovered between sailing a small sailboat and leading a team is that to lead a team I had to be able to clearly articulate the destination. On my own, I could just pick my tac on the horizon and set sail, but with a team, if everyone doesn't precisely know where we are going, we are headed for trouble.

Preparing for the launch of *I Didn't Like Hubert* I discovered this the hard way. Not only did the product itself fail, but the launch event was almost the end of me. As we were doing this passion project on the side of our paid commercial work, I didn't want to take up more time from the team than necessary. Subsequently, I didn't take enough time to stop and articulate my vision for the launch to my colleagues. I didn't tell them the story of where we were going, I didn't create an opportunity for the team to get buy-in, or articulate what success looked like and I certainly hadn't taken the time to delegate out proper roles or responsibilities. This meant only one thing: everything fell back onto my shoulders.

So a couple of days out from launch, I found myself running around late at night trying to organise sound equipment, cutting out painted backdrops, booking in catering, packing gift bags, managing RSVPs, picking up bags of ice, and lining up a video greeting from our celebrity LA-based narrator. My team wanted to help, but I hadn't empowered them to take ownership of the vision with me and proactively contribute in any way. I had set the tac on the horizon and set sail off by myself. I needed to have shared the vision with the team and then headed off on the journey with them.

Needless to say, the day after we launched *Hubert*, I fell into a heap and stayed there for some time. And in the subsequent days, the miserable sales performance from the app itself didn't help to bolster my spirits. Our launch would have been much better had I taken the time to cast the vision and allow my team the time to get onboard and make it their own.

TAKEAWAYS

Determine the destination and then work with the conditions to get there. The journey to our destinations is rarely an easy straight path, but embracing the real world conditions we can not just get through, but harness the challenges to propel us forward.

Good leaders clearly articulate the destination to those around them. If everyone on the team doesn't know where you are heading, you are headed for trouble.

CHAPTER NINETEEN | **MISSION DRIFT**

The Man Who Chases Two Rabbits Catches Neither

Boy, did that hurt the first time I read those famous words from Confucius: 'The man who chases two rabbits, catches neither.'

The leader pursuing two visions ends up achieving none of them.

As you could probably guess, these words hurt because I was pursuing two visions. Five years into starting Taste Creative, we had mission drift. We'd allowed the current to take us off course and when I did look up to realign with our destination, I found that we were not where I wanted to be, and there were two things that I was pursuing. With our origins in storytelling and film production, our vision was creating a production company with work so excellent that it spoke for itself. Think Walt Disney, Aardman Animations, Studio Ghibli, Pixar. But, at the same time, we had grown in response to our clients' requests. Companies were so happy with our film production work that they'd ask for our help designing a new logo, building their website or designing their trade-show graphics. And being dutiful business owners with a modus operandi to grow (and the pressure to cover our rent and staff salaries), we'd say 'Yes'.

Within five years of starting, we found ourselves building a micro-creative agency. In addition to our film production, we were now offering strategy, animation, design and digital to our clients. We had built a strong team of film editors, art directors, producers, animators, designers, web developers, client managers and strategists, ramped up our own marketing to reposition ourselves as a 'one-stop-shop' and set up a prestigiously large creative studio in central Sydney. Our incoming leads had increased, but so too had our costs. I soon found myself spending 90% of my time chasing any work opportunities a client could give us just to sustain the overheads. We were swimming in profitless prosperity.

Meanwhile, we continued to pursue our vision of producing high-quality film production. The result was a diluted and confusing offering to our clients. On the one hand, we were saying that we were high-end film specialists and, on the other, we were a 'jack of all trades' that could do anything creative that they needed. One strategy was narrow and specific, the other was broad and shallow.

I'm very grateful to have a number of clients that we have built strong personal relationships with. It was with one of these wonderful clients who knew our business well, possibly better than we did at that point, who I asked, over dinner, for an outsider's viewpoint. We had worked with Narelle for quite a few years and her opinion had become one I greatly trusted, so I wanted to see the value of what we had to offer through her eyes.

Narelle highlighted to me the reasons they enjoyed working with us and continued to come back, project after project. And it wasn't because we were offering to do everything. In fact, they had specialised agencies for all their design and digital needs. They even had creative agencies that could produce their video and animation needs if they needed it.

But it was the high-end storytelling that they looked to us for. The ability to not just create film content, but to be able to deeply engage with their audience on an emotional level.

Here was our unique asset.

As I looked deeper, it turned out that the types of clients who wanted a one-stop-shop solution from us were not interested in paying very much, so the jobs weren't highly profitable. They were usually organisations who required a lot of hands-on time, wanted multiple rounds of additional changes and rarely had enough budget to cover what they really needed.

Ultimately my choice was simple: did we want to be mediocre at lots of things, or excellent at one thing? It was time for us to stop, recalibrate and commit to chasing just one rabbit.

Next we had to work out the right time. There is a danger in pulling the trigger at the wrong time and have everything fall over. Remember the lemon tree I fastidiously nurtured? As it had been lovingly gifted to me by my grandma, I had taken great care to ensure it moved with us from house to house. It was a delicate tree. Each year it would offer us up a small but delicious harvest of lemons. As we were preparing for an upcoming house move, I knew the tree was overdue to be repotted into a much larger pot. Its roots needed the space to stretch out to allow for its next season of growth. But the lemon tree was covered in green fruit that was just about to turn yellow and become ripe. If I had repotted it then, very likely the tree wouldn't have survived the move and would have died within weeks. It wouldn't be able to re-establish itself quickly enough in a new pot to get the nutrients it needed from the soil for its large harvest. Right circumstances, wrong time. I just had to wait until the harvest had finished and then the tree would be able to enjoy its new, much roomier pot.

Similarly in our business, I had to wait until it was the right circumstances and right time. Fortunately, I didn't have to wait too long. A couple of weeks later, many projects were coming to a natural conclusion and new jobs hadn't yet kicked off. It was time to start pruning. Like with my beloved lemon tree, I needed to prune back the branches that were not producing good fruit to see good growth in the future.

So I got out my metaphoric secateurs and started to prune our business right back. We immediately started saying no to requests for websites and design work, we reframed our marketing to showcase our strong storytelling skills and we started to let go of the less profitable clients that were taking up a lot of our time. Saying no to paying work was tough, especially when there are bills to pay every week, but we knew that we had to get back to a singular vision of chasing one rabbit and not be pulled in multiple directions.

I was very grateful for Narelle's viewpoint for she could see what we couldn't. I was reminded of this years later when I was working on a film with Australian tennis great Dylan Alcott. He had just announced his retirement after becoming Australia's number one wheelchair tennis player. Even then, at the top of his game, he had still been working diligently with his tennis coach. 'Surely you don't still need a coach, do you?' I jokingly asked. 'There can't be much more to teach you.' Dylan laughed. 'Unfortunately I can't see my posture from behind when I serve,' he responded. 'But my coach can!'

Even the best sportspeople need someone they trust to see their blind spots.

TAKEAWAYS

The leader pursuing two visions ends up achieving none of them. Growing in response to clients' requests can lead to a diluted and confusing offering.

Wait for the right timings for the big changes. Repotting a plant in the wrong season doesn't set it up for success. But when the time is right, pruning non-productive branches can lead to transformational growth in the future.

CHAPTER TWENTY | **CREATIVE SURVIVAL**

Learning How to Live. Really Live.

Sitting in a conference room in late 2017, the former CEO of Facebook Australia, Stephen Scheeler, asked the room; 'What does a tsunami feel like if you're sitting in a boat way out on the ocean?' As I sat there, I pictured scenes from *The Perfect Storm*: crashing waves, torrential wind, you know ... general terror. In fact it's quite the opposite. A tsunami is at its maximum destructiveness as it crashes to land, but out on the ocean, before it reaches the shore, it will feel like just a blip underneath the boat, a small ripple as it starts to build momentum and races towards the land.

As leaders, it's important that we don't spend all of our time standing on the beach alongside the crowds. We must position ourselves a few kilometres out on the ocean in the little boat. From the boat, we have the gift of time to feel those warning signs when something threatening may come along, and be in a better position to do something about it and hopefully avoid catastrophe.

In early 2020, like countless leaders around the world, I felt that small ripple.

Preparing to celebrate the ten year anniversary of our production company, we began 2020 with a busy team who all commuted into the city to the studio each day. Like so many other companies, meetings were held in conference rooms, we would catch the train across town for project meetings and fly interstate to meet with out-of-town clients. This is what I, and most of the world, felt business was. Anything less was seen as not professional, not productive and not efficient.

Within a couple of days of Australians being casually cautioned about Covid-19 in February 2020, we had decided to take no risks and instructed our staff to pack up their desks and set up at home for the week. As a team, we had encouraged a flexible working environment so this new work style wasn't foreign, but external perceptions of the need for in-person client meetings had prevented us from making this the norm. My thinking was to take a week to fully pressure test this remote office model, test the limitations and adjust accordingly. Then we'd all come back with a fail-safe backup plan at the ready, just in case.

We moved every meeting and conversation online, we ironed out the kinks of our IT systems (this was a tricky challenge, particularly for teams collaborating on large film edits), we ensured everyone had ergonomic desk setups, we familiarised ourselves with each other's home dynamics of children, partners and interrupting pets, and we began working through how we would retain the wonderful person-first culture we had spent so many years creating in the office.

By day three of our week-long trial, with new information rapidly coming out about the seriousness of Covid-19, I called the team together and informed them that we would not be returning to the office for some time. A couple of weeks, a couple of months—we weren't sure at the time.

Fast forward to today and the world, of course, looks very different. Fundamentally, the stigma around the reliability of communications via video calls and the productivity of staff working from home has been irreversibly challenged and for the better. For me, I've loved the ability to work as flexibly as we are now. The capacity to meet with more people thanks to heavily reduced transit times, more focused work with fewer interruptions and a global refocusing on a healthier work/life balance, this was Oliver Burkeman's 'Great Pause' in full effect.

But the downsides have been difficult. Losing the spontaneous in-person culture has been sad—sitting out in the sun with the team for lunch, joking around in the office, downtime with team members between projects, and the magic of collaboration when you're sitting next to someone.

The uncertainty the pandemic caused for our clients meant 90% of our work was put on hold indefinitely. Each client sector was affected differently, but everyone was nervous. Our incoming revenue stopped almost overnight and our future pipeline froze. We backflipped and manoeuvred projects to carve out new pathways to be able to continue producing film and animation content in the new environment.

We even managed to safely film a three-part TV series in multiple states at the height of Australia's first (of many) lockdowns.

Letting go of our team as all of our work dried up was the most brutal chapter we had yet experienced. After fifteen months of grit and survival, Genevieve and I dialled into a team video call with tears in our eyes and broke the news that we would have to let everyone go. We had sustained it for as long as we could, but we had been haemorrhaging cash to stay afloat and the ship would soon sink if we stayed on this course. Everyone had always known this as a reality, but the team was crushed. We had created a very strong family-like culture of care for each other, so to break this apart was excruciatingly difficult.

A real kindness at this time was that we had been able to farewell each other face-to-face. A week after our in-person farewell lunch, Australia was plunged into another lockdown, this time for four long months.

In the Bible, a physician called Luke shares some good advice. He says: 'Use every adversity to stimulate you to creative survival, to concentrate your attention on the bare essentials, so you'll live, really live, and not complacently just get by on good behaviour.' He said this more than 1,900 years ago, yet the wisdom is just as timely.

My image of leadership was incredibly challenged. I used to spend the majority of my time leading a core team of creatives and a large collective of freelancers to achieve great things every day and now I had no team to lead. My focus needed to come back to the bare essentials. I had to activate my creative survival.

Today, my days don't consist of staff meetings, management WIPs or team appraisals. I don't commute to an office and it is only infrequently that I sit in the same room as our clients.

What I do have is the gift of time. To lead well is to draw from the well of experiences that we are fortunate enough to accumulate along the journey. But even after over a decade of leading a production company (I may have surpassed the 10,000 hours of Malcolm Gladwell's theory to become an expert in something), I certainly do not feel I have mastered leadership. There is always something else to uncover.

Three months after letting our team go, Genevieve and my little family grew exponentially with the birth of our identical twin girls, Monet and Everest. Born one month premature and with Genevieve overcoming a few health complications, I was overwhelmed with pride as I drove my family home for our first night released from the hospital and out in the big world.

Those first weeks were spent very much in the deep end, learning how to be parents, and with two infants at the same time. Before our girls arrived, we had read plenty of handbooks, spoke to countless parents and did all the courses you're supposed to, but nothing can prepare you for being a parent. We were freefalling out of the plane and learning how to build the parachute on the way down.

But this time, we had already done it before.

Acknowledgments

This book was never meant to be a book.

I realise this is a strange way to start the acknowledgments. At the start of Covid-19, I thought I would jot down some of my stories and illustrations to share with my teammates and people I mentor to encourage them with some of the wisdom that I have been gifted on my journey. I am grateful for the people who encouraged me to bring them to life as a book.

Tracy, I am very thankful that you took the time to impart your wisdom of the psychology of writing a book. To hear someone say that we don't write to become rich and famous but to share the things we love put wind in my sails.

Tony and Mark, I am so touched by the efforts you went to in helping shape this book into what it is today. Iron sharpens iron, and your support, suggestions and honest feedback was exactly what I needed.

Ann, thank you for your constant championing of entrepreneurship and supporting the next wave of purpose-led leaders coming up through the ranks.

Thank you, Jessica and Angela, for your amazing grammatical guidance. Because of you, readers will never know that I'm not a perfect writer*.

Wendy, Geoff, Brian and Helen, not just great mentors to Genevieve and I, but godparents to Monet and Everest. I am grateful for all that you have poured into us both.

And thank you to my darling wife, Genevieve, who has been supportive of this idea from my very first early morning writing session.

---

* Well I guess now you will. Ten points to you if you read this far.

About the Author

Henry Smith is an award-winning entrepreneur and filmmaker. Having collaborated with clients around the world including National Geographic, Sesame Street, Unilever and Google, Henry has a wealth of knowledge when it comes to starting and running a business with purpose.

But what sets Henry apart is his commitment to inclusivity and diversity in the film industry. As a passionate champion for the inclusion of people living with disability, he co-established Inclusively Made, a global standard of inclusion in commercial production and film making.

How to Jump Without a Parachute shares Henry's insights and expertise on how to lead with authenticity and embrace diversity in the workplace, guiding entrepreneurs towards success while making a positive impact on the world.